FBI CASE
FILES
MICHIGAN

FBI CASE FILES MICHIGAN

TALES OF A G-MAN

Greg Stejskal

Published by The History Press
Charleston, SC
www.historypress.com

Copyright © 2021 by Greg Stejskal
All rights reserved

FBI badge image (*author's collection*) used with permission of the FBI.

First published 2021

Manufactured in the United States

ISBN 9781467148900

Library of Congress Control Number: 2021934590

Notice: The information in this book is true and complete to the best of our knowledge. It is offered without guarantee on the part of the author or The History Press. The author and The History Press disclaim all liability in connection with the use of this book.

All rights reserved. No part of this book may be reproduced or transmitted in any form whatsoever without prior written permission from the publisher except in the case of brief quotations embodied in critical articles and reviews.

To my parents who, by example, helped me calibrate the declination to true north on my moral compass.

And to Pat, "Spanky," my wife, a steadfast friend and romantic partner in the great adventure of life.

CONTENTS

Acknowledgements 9
Introduction 11

1. Reporting to Detroit, and Jimmy Hoffa Disappears 15
2. Somebody Is Poisoning Patients: Murders at the Ann Arbor
    Veterans Hospital 22
3. The Telltale Fingerprints 30
4. A Detroit Mob Photograph by the FBI Surveillance Squad
    Captures History 36
5. Kidnapping for Ransom: A Bad Business Model 43
6. The Double Steal: Theft of Flat Glass Technology 50
7. The Annual Talk with the Michigan Football Team About
    Sports Gambling 55
8. Print the Fact: How the Unabomber Was First Identified 59
9. The FBI Gets Jurisdiction to Investigate Drug Trafficking 65
10. A Tale of a GM Executive Who Got Busted Selling Test Cars 72
11. Unmasking the Joker 76
12. A Cuban Inmate Uprising, the Salvation Army
    and Santa's Helper 82
13. 3:10 to Marquette: A Manhunt in the Northwoods
    of Michigan 86
14. Mark from Michigan: The Rise and Fall of a Founder of
    the Michigan Militia Movement 94

Contents

15. A Tale of Union Racketeering or How I Learned to Love the Hobbs Act	99
16. They Shoot Horses, Don't They?	104
17. Is It OK to Shout Fire in a Crowded Chat Room?: A Michigan Case that Tested Free Speech in the Early Days of the Internet	113
18. The History of April 19: American Revolution, Waco and the Oklahoma City Bombing	119
19. The Tale of the Stolen Meteorite: Almost an X-File	126
20. The Hole-in-the-Truck Gang	131
21. A Happy Ending for Law Enforcement in a Spa Crackdown	136
22. Robin Hood in Reverse: A $1.1 Million Scam	140
23. Retirement and a Cold Murder Case in Detroit Dating Back to 1857	143
Bibliography	149
Index	151
About the Author	157

ACKNOWLEDGEMENTS

I want to thank Allan Lengel, the editor of *Deadline Detroit*, an online newspaper, and *Tickle-the-Wire*, a federal law enforcement blog. After I retired from the bureau, he asked me to write a recurring column for *Tickle*. He had the patience to help me write a column that didn't sound like an FD 302, an FBI document reporting a summary of an interview—not exactly literature.

Also, thanks to John Hilton, the editor of the *Ann Arbor Observer*, a monthly magazine. John has supported my writing efforts and published some of my stories.

And to all the people who read and/or heard my stories and asked me when I was going to write a book—you asked for it.

INTRODUCTION

This is not an autobiography or a memoir. It is a compilation of stories from my perspective about cases I was involved in during my over-thirty-year career in the FBI, which was almost all in Michigan. Although this is not a book about me, I thought it would interest readers to know how I became an FBI agent.

My mother and father met when my father was stationed at Fort Lewis in Washington during World War II. My mother had graduated with honors from the University of Washington. They married before my father shipped out. He was a lieutenant in the combat engineers with General Patton's Third Army from their landing in France until VE Day. (He was awarded the Silver Star for valor in an action in Luxembourg.) In 1944, while my father was in Europe, my older brother, Richard, was born. After the war, my parents moved to Omaha, Nebraska, my father's hometown. He returned to the cattle business, where he had worked prior to the war. (He remained in the army reserve and retired a lieutenant colonel.)

I was born in 1949 and grew up in an older middle-class neighborhood with a lot of kids. (It was the baby boom.) I have fond memories of my childhood. We spent a lot of time outside doing all kinds of activities—little of it organized, except by us kids. But every Friday evening, we would rush home to watch *Superman* on TV and revel in his fight "for truth, justice and the American way." It was the 1950s, and despite being in the midst of the Cold War, life seemed simpler and carefree, at least where I lived.

Introduction

My younger brother, James, was born in 1954. Our mother stayed home but was a strong advocate for public education and became the state president of the Parent Teacher Association. When my brothers and I were older, she earned a doctorate of education degree and was an elementary and secondary principal in the Omaha Public Schools.

My brothers and I were active in Boy Scouts with strong support from our parents. We all earned the rank of Eagle Scout. Scouting had a great impact on me. In addition to the usual scout skills, scouting gave me an abiding appreciation and love for my country and core values like honor and integrity.

When I was in the fifth grade, I read a Landmark book (a series of books for young readers published by Random House), *The FBI*. Then I saw the movie *The FBI Story* with Jimmy Stewart. From then on, I wanted to be an FBI agent.

Being an adolescent in the 1960s was a little more difficult. I went to high school at Omaha Central, the oldest high school in Nebraska. It was located downtown but drew students from all over the city. It was solely a college preparatory school with high academic standards and a racially and ethnically diverse student body. Over the years, Omaha Central has turned out some outstanding alumni. I was a better-than-average student, but my main interest was football. When I graduated in 1967, I went to the University of Nebraska in Lincoln (UNL) on a football scholarship.

Nebraska was a football power then (the Nebraska University football team was the national champion in 1970 and 1971). I was a pretty good football player but not good enough to play for the best program in the country, and my football career waned. But my desire to be an FBI agent did not. I was accepted into the Nebraska College of Law. (At the time, the best way to get into the FBI was to be an attorney.) For the first time, I became a very serious student, because success in law school required it. I also acquired a greater respect for the law and the Constitution.

In 1974, as I neared graduation from law school, I submitted my application to the FBI. I graduated with honors, took the bar exam and passed it. While I was waiting to hear from the bureau, I worked as a special deputy U.S. Marshal doing courtroom security. That fall, the FBI advised me that I had been accepted, and I was to report for duty in Washington, D.C., on March 10, 1975.

On March 1, 1975, I married Patricia, née Legate, who I had met while we were both in school at UNL. When we were married, she was working as a flight attendant with United Airlines. Our honeymoon was abbreviated,

Introduction

Lobby card from the 1959 movie *The FBI Story*. Jimmy Stewart signed it for me after I became an agent. *Author's collection.*

and we were only together a few times while I was in new agent training at Quantico, Virginia.

On March 10, I reported to the Department of Justice building in Washington, D.C., referred to as "Main Justice," to be sworn in as a special agent of the FBI with my fellow new agents. In a large room that had been used for the secret trial of the Nazi saboteurs during World War II (a story I first read about in that Landmark book), I raised my right hand and took the oath that every agent takes:

> *I* [name] *do solemnly swear that I will support and defend the Constitution of the United States against all enemies, foreign and domestic; that I will bear true faith and allegiance to the same; that I take this obligation freely, without any mental reservation or purpose of evasion; that I will well and faithfully discharge the duties of the office on which I am about to enter. So help me God.*

Introduction

Unlike those Nazi saboteurs who swore an oath to the Fuhrer, we swore allegiance to the concept that the United States is a country of laws and that no person is above the law. We were not taking an oath of fealty to anyone.

After completing my new agent training at Quantico, I had an almost thirty-two-year career investigating and prosecuting violations of federal laws. I was involved in hundreds of cases—many of them high-profile. There are stories connected to all of these cases. In this book, I have compiled what I believe are some of the best stories—at least the ones that I can tell. Although I wrote these stories in the first person and sometimes use singular pronouns, I want to emphasize that I accomplished nothing in my career by myself. The FBI, often with the help of other federal agencies and state and local law enforcement, is a team. Everything is a team effort. It was a great honor for me to be part of that team.

I'm just telling the stories.

1

REPORTING TO DETROIT, AND JIMMY HOFFA DISAPPEARS

The FBI's new agent training is conducted at the FBI Academy, a sprawling complex located in the backwoods of the Quantico, Virginia Marine Corps Base, about forty miles south of Washington, D.C. My class's new agent training was fourteen weeks long, and at about the twelfth week, we were told what our first office of assignment would be. Mine was Detroit—little did I know that it was to be my only office. There was some trepidation, as neither my wife nor I had ever been to Detroit, and we didn't know anyone there.

Detroit is one of fifty-six field offices or divisions of the FBI in the United States, and Detroit Division's territory covers the entire state of Michigan. There are branch offices that are called resident agencies (RAs) spread across the state in Grand Rapids, Lansing, Flint, Ann Arbor, Marquette and several other cities.

My training ended in June 1975, and later that month, I reported to the Detroit field office. Not wanting to be late on my first day and being unfamiliar with Detroit, I got up extra early and drove to the office. I was in the office around 6:00 a.m. The only other people in the office were the night supervisor, an agent in charge of the night shift and a few support people. (There is a skeleton staff in field offices 24/7. This was more important before the advent of computers and cellphones.) The night supervisor was an old-timer who regaled me with stories from his career in the bureau.

Since I was about two hours early, I was able to have a long conversation with the night supervisor before going to the front office to officially report to the special agent in charge (SAC). Each field office has a SAC, except the exceptionally large offices that are run by assistant directors. The SAC of the Detroit office was Neil Welch. Welch was notorious in the bureau. He was known for trying to maintain his field office's independence from FBI headquarters (FBIHQ), and because of that, there were those at FBIHQ who viewed Welch as a rogue SAC. Welch's investigative priority was organized crime (OC), which, at that time, meant the La Cosa Nostra (LCN) or Mafia. He established the first FBI surveillance squad that was primarily tasked with collecting intelligence on the Detroit Mafia "family" (more about that in chapter 4). Later, Welch was the assistant director in charge of the New York City field office. The NYC office prosecuted some major OC and public corruption cases under his leadership. (The Abdul Scam, or ABSCAM, case was one of his cases. The movie *American Hustle* was loosely based on the ABSCAM case.)

Welch was not known for his warm personality. When I was ushered into his office, he was reading the newspaper, and I am not sure he stopped reading to welcome me. He told me that because I was a new agent, I would be assigned to the fugitive squad. He did pay me what I took to be a compliment by saying that he hoped to have me work OC once I was more experienced.

The fugitive squad was a great learning ground. The investigations were relatively simple—tracking down fugitives. At that time, the FBI had broad authority to arrest various categories of fugitives who were wanted for violating federal laws. But some of the most interesting and challenging fugitives were those who the FBI called UFAPs (unlawful flight to avoid prosecution). These were fugitives who had been charged by a state for committing serious crimes and then believed to have fled that state to avoid prosecution. Often, the UFAP fugitives had been charged with murder. (Chapter 3 contains a story about one such investigation.)

I had been in Detroit for about a month when, on July 31, 1975, the FBI learned that Jimmy Hoffa (James Riddle Hoffa), the former president of the International Brotherhood of Teamsters, had disappeared the day before. The disappearance immediately drew national attention. In investigations of this nature, there is usually a short window of opportunity. All available Detroit agents, including me, were called in to aid in the investigation. Hoffa was last seen in the parking lot outside the Machus Red Fox restaurant, and his car was found there. The Machus Red Fox was in Bloomfield Township, a suburb in Oakland County, north of Detroit. In what is termed a "neighborhood investigation," the area in and

Jimmy Hoffa (*left*) and his Teamster vice president, Frank Fitzsimmons, at a rally for striking truck drivers in 1965. *Courtesy of the Walter Reuther Library, Wayne State University.*

around the restaurant was flooded with agents trying to find witnesses who might have seen something. Agents talked to employees and customers at the restaurant. It was difficult to identify many of the early afternoon customers from July 30, as many had paid with cash. Some were known to the employees or had made reservations. (Credit card use was not as prevalent in 1975. I have often thought that we might have had more success had there been cellphone GPS data available or the now seemingly ubiquitous security camera–recorded images.)

Six people had seen Hoffa in the parking lot, and five of the six talked to him. Hoffa never intended to go into the restaurant, and he apparently did not. The restaurant required a jacket and tie, and Hoffa had not brought either with him. One witness saw Hoffa talking to three men in a car, and another witness saw him get into the backseat of the car. The car was described as a maroon Lincoln or Mercury, and the witnesses thought this activity occurred between 2:30 and 3:00 p.m. It was also established that Hoffa had called home between 2:15 and 2:30 p.m. from a pay phone outside of a hardware store next to the restaurant and asked his wife, Josephine, if Tony Giacalone had called. He told his wife that he was supposed to meet Tony Giacalone at 2:00 p.m. but that he had not arrived. It was estimated that Hoffa had left the parking lot in someone else's car between 2:50 p.m.

and 3:00 p.m. At Hoffa's home, a note was found on his desk that read, "TG—230pm Wed 14 Mile Tel Fox Rest Maple Road." (The time on the note was probably a mistake, as Hoffa told several people that the meeting was at 2:00 p.m.). A rudimentary timeline had been established, and we knew who set him up and why. What we did not have was any evidence of a murder, and there was no body. There's a legal axiom that a murder cannot be proved without a body. That is not always true, but it almost always is.

After the initial investigation, it became a more traditional investigation, involving fewer agents interviewing Hoffa's family, associates, friends, enemies and informants. A federal grand jury was used, and between September and December 1975, ninety-five individuals appeared before it. Of these individuals, twenty-two exercised their Fifth Amendment privilege and refused to testify. The people who refused to testify were either known LCN members or Teamster officials—or both. The two original case agents were Robert "Bob" Garrity and James "Jim" Esposito, both seasoned OC agents. They understood the dynamics of the relationship between the Teamsters and the Mafia and how it came to be.

Jimmy Hoffa was working as a truck driver in Detroit when, in 1931, he helped organize a strike of loading dock workers who off-loaded the trucks that delived produce to Kroger Grocery and Baking Co. in Detroit. Around that time, Hoffa joined the International Brotherhood of the Teamsters (a term originally used for wagon drivers). The Teamsters Union was established for truck drivers and other workers in the trucking industry. After joining the Teamsters, Hoffa became an organizer for the union and began his meteoric rise within it. He became president of Teamsters Local 299 in Detroit. In 1957, Hoffa became the national president of the Teamsters and was primarily responsible for making it the most dominant union in the country.

Hoffa also developed a symbiotic relationship with the Mafia. Initially, the Mafia connection was concentrated in Detroit, but it involved nationwide activity. As an interconnected nationwide organization, the Mafia provided Hoffa and the Teamsters with muscle and entrance into various businesses, like construction and trash hauling. In return, Hoffa gave the Mafia access to the Teamsters' large pension fund. The Mafia used this access to invest in casinos and hotels in Las Vegas, using front people so as not to disclose their involvement. These extremely profitable investments resulted in lucrative returns for both the Mafia and the Teamsters.

In addition to his questionable relationship with the Mafia, some of Hoffa's other union-related activities were illegal. In 1967, Hoffa was sent to prison on federal charges of fraud, bribery and jury tampering. Hoffa was forced to cede the Teamsters presidency to his handpicked vice president, Frank Fitzsimmons. Even in prison, Hoffa retained his popularity with much of the Teamsters' rank and file. He also continued to wield some control over union affairs. On his release from prison in 1972, Hoffa began a campaign to regain control of what he regarded as his union. But Frank Fitzsimmons did not want to step down. He had gained some autonomy by being elected as president in his own right while Hoffa was in prison; also, his Mafia sponsors were comfortable with having the much-more-malleable Fitzsimmons in charge.

As Hoffa's frustration grew, he started making not-so-subtle threats that he would expose the Mafia-Teamsters financial relationship. It is suspected that Hoffa orchestrated the bombing of Fitzsimmons's son's car in the parking lot at Nemo's Bar on July 10, 1975. Fitzsimmons and his son Richard were in Nemo's when the car bomb exploded. Nemo's was located a few blocks from the old Detroit Tiger's stadium, and it was a few blocks farther from Teamsters Local 299, Hoffa's and Fitzsimmons's home local. Nemo's was a regular hangout for Teamsters officers. (Coincidentally, it was also frequented by FBI agents, especially on Fridays after work.) If

The Machus Red Fox Restaurant in Bloomfield Township, Michigan, as it looked on the day Jimmy Hoffa disappeared, July 30, 1975. *Courtesy of the Walter Reuther Library, Wayne State University.*

Hoffa was responsible for the bombing, it is not clear whether he intended to kill Fitzsimmons or just warn him.

On July 26, Anthony "Tony" Giacalone and Vito "Billy Jack" Giacalone, both capos (short for *caporegime*, or captain) in the Detroit Mafia family, met with Hoffa at his residence in Lake Orion. Tony Giacalone was the primary Mafia liaison with the Teamsters. It is not known what was discussed at this meeting, but it presumably involved Hoffa's desire to regain control of the Teamsters and the threats he had made. Another meeting was scheduled for July 30. Hoffa believed he was to meet with Tony Giacalone—and possibly others—outside the Machus Red Fox. We know that Hoffa was there at the appointed time, but Tony Giacalone was not. Giacalone made a considerable effort to make sure people knew he was at the Southfield Athletic Club (several miles from the Machus) on the afternoon of July 30.

After Hoffa was seen getting into the backseat of a car in the restaurant parking lot, it is not known what happened to him. He was most likely killed and his body destroyed as quickly as possible. The Mafia was particularly good at making people disappear, but this was probably the most prominent, well-known person they had ever eliminated. The probable motive for Hoffa's murder was his threat to expose the Teamster-Mafia relationship.

The FBI's investigation continued for years after Hoffa's disappearance. In 1982, Hoffa was declared legally dead.

Although no one was ever charged with his murder and his body was never found, there is relative certainty about who was involved in the murder and why it happened.

The Mafia was successful in eliminating a threat to their very lucrative relationship with the Teamsters and the union's pension fund. The Mafia must have known that killing Hoffa would result in tremendous investigative pressure, which it did. The mob probably thought that by disposing of Hoffa's body in a way that it could never be found, limiting the number of people who had knowledge of his murder and practicing omerta, the Mafia code of silence, they could weather the resulting investigation. To that extent, they were successful, but their goal of retaining access to the Teamsters pension fund was short-lived.

The FBI investigation of the Hoffa disappearance resulted in scrutiny of the corruption within the Teamsters. Ultimately, the Teamsters were temporarily placed under federal control, and many of the union's officers were convicted of labor racketeering–related charges, including Frank Fitzsimmons's son Richard, who had become the vice president of the Detroit Local 299. (Ironically, Jimmy Hoffa's son, James P. Hoffa, ultimately became the national president of the Teamsters after the union was substantially purged of corruption.)

Between 1996 and 1998, the hierarchy of the Detroit Mafia family were prosecuted and convicted for violations of the Racketeering Influenced and Corrupt Organization Act (RICO). Some of the predicate acts that established a RICO case involved the Detroit family's "secret" acquisition of casinos in Nevada. In the 1960s and 1970s, those acquisitions used money from the Teamsters pension fund. The hierarchy included both Tony and Vito Giacalone. Vito Giacalone pleaded guilty prior to the trial. Tony Giacalone, who had previously been convicted of tax evasion in 1976, never stood trial due to severe medical problems. He died from heart failure in 2001.

2

SOMEBODY IS POISONING PATIENTS

Murders at the Ann Arbor Veterans Hospital

When you have eliminated all which is impossible, then whatever remains, however improbable, must be the truth.
—Sherlock Holmes, Sir Arthur Conan Doyle

A few weeks after Hoffa disappeared, about twenty agents, including me, were sent to Ann Arbor as a task force to investigate multiple deaths from apparent poisoning at the Ann Arbor Veterans Hospital. (The Department of Justice and the FBI had jurisdiction because veterans hospitals are federal facilities.) The case was a classic "whodunit," and its resolution was worthy of Hercule Poirot or Sherlock Holmes.

If this had been a fictional mystery story, the hospital would have been a dark, foreboding place, but it was not. The Ann Arbor Veterans Administration Hospital (VAH) was built in 1953 of reddish brick, and it had generic governmental architecture. It sits on a hill above the meandering Huron River and on the edge of the north campus of the University of Michigan. This placid scene belied the events that occurred there during the summer of 1975.

During a six-week period that summer, there was a sudden spike of patients experiencing breathing failures that required emergency resuscitation (termed code 7 emergencies within the VAH). Initially, the medical staff was not overly concerned, as such resuscitations are routine—albeit not as frequent as they were beginning to experience. But as the incidents continued to become more frequent, the staff became alarmed. Some of the patients could not be revived and died as a result.

One staff member, Dr. Anne Hill, an Irish-born chief of anesthesiology, was not only concerned but also began to suspect foul play. On August 15, her suspicion coalesced into a conclusion that someone was intentionally poisoning patients. On that day, there were three respiratory failures within twenty minutes—each resulting in a code 7 alert and requiring emergency resuscitation. Dr. Hill was present for all three of the code 7 resuscitations. On seeing the first victim, she determined that, based on their symptoms—being in a flaccid state but with a pulse—the patient had been administered a powerful muscle relaxant. After doing some diagnostic tests, she concluded that the drug Pavulon (pancuronium bromide) had been given to the patient. (Pavulon is the synthetic equivalent of curare, a plant-derived toxin that was used by some South American Natives to poison the tips of their blowgun darts and arrows.) Within minutes of being administered, Pavulon causes muscles to be deactivated, including the muscles used for breathing. The victim remains conscious but is paralyzed and suffocates. To test her conclusion, Dr. Hill gave the patient an antidote for Pavulon, which immediately alleviated the victim's breathing failure. Dr. Hill was able to further test her conclusion with the next two code 7 incidents.

Based on Dr. Hill's discovery, a call was made to the FBI, the agency responsible for investigating crimes in VA hospitals, as they are federal facilities. That very night, Gene Ward, an agent from the FBI Ann Arbor Office (resident agency) went to the VAH. After being briefed and assessing the situation, Agent Ward called an Assistant U.S. Attorney (AUSA), Richard "Dick" Delonis, and said, "Dick you're not going to believe this, but—." The poisonings ended that day, but it was the beginning of an arduous and, in some ways, groundbreaking investigation that would last for over a year. The FBI responded by sending a task force of agents to investigate.

This case was unique—a huge understatement—but it would be pursued by the numbers. First, however, investigators would have to prove that a crime had taken place. Were the respiratory arrests caused by the intentional and illicit administration of the muscle relaxant Pavulon? But there was an immediate problem. The patients for whom the emergency resuscitation had been unsuccessful were dead and buried. The bodies would have to be exhumed and tested for Pavulon. There was a further complication, as there was no existing test for Pavulon in the tissue of a corpse after the embalming process. The FBI Laboratory was tasked with developing a test that would be defensible in court. The laboratory developed a test, and some of the corpses of the presumed poisoning victims were exhumed. Traces of Pavulon were found in their tissue.

The case also involved the observations of the medical staff who were involved in the emergency resuscitations. Pavulon's effects are relatively easy to identify. When administered in undiluted doses, it creates an effect on the body that is virtually unique to muscle relaxants: the individual's heart continues to beat while their breathing stops. (There is no known disease process that has ever been shown to cause this phenomenon.)

Most of the suspected victims were patients in the intensive care unit (ICU) who were being continuously monitored. Thus, the investigators were able to identify fifty-one suspicious breathing failures. This number was cut to thirty-eight respiratory arrests, which the FBI believed was the minimum number of poisonings. Some of the patients/victims were poisoned more than once, and at least nine died as a result. VAH records showed that no Pavulon had been prescribed to any of the victims.

Early on, it was determined that for the Pavulon to cause complete and rapid respiratory arrest, it had to be administered, undiluted, directly into the victim's intravenous (IV) tube, a so-called bolus injection. This would have caused breathing failure in less than three minutes. This finding was critical in narrowing the window of opportunity from when the poisoner injected the Pavulon to when breathing failure began. Later, this finding of the two- to three-minute interval was the keystone to the ultimate prosecution of the case. At trial, the defense recognized this and attempted to suggest that a longer interval was possible.

To further bolster the two- to three-minute interval at trial, the prosecution used the testimony of a pathologist and world-renowned authority on muscle relaxants, Dr. Francis Foldes, a Hungarian American. (If this were a movie, Dr. Foldes would have come from central casting—accent, tweed coat and all.) Dr. Foldes literally wrote the book on the subject, *Muscle Relaxants In Anesthesiology*. Although the defense brought their own expert to challenge Dr. Foldes's conclusions, they presented no evidence to challenge Dr. Foldes's statements. Dr. Foldes testified that the victims were poisoned by an injection of Pavulon that was injected directly into the victims' IV tubes. It would not have had the devastating effect it did had it been introduced in its diluted form (say, if it had been injected into the IV bottle). Finally, Dr. Foldes testified that the respiratory arrest would have occurred within three minutes of the injection.

Returning to the investigation, the agents had to determine who had been in the position to inject Pavulon into the patients/victims within

Tales of a G-Man

A 1981 retrospective of the veterans hospital murder case that appeared in the *Detroit Free Press. Courtesy of the* Detroit Free Press.

the three minutes prior to them going into respiratory arrest. This was a difficult process because it required the reconstruction of each of the dozens of poisonings. Over 750 people who were in the VAH at the time of the poisonings were questioned by the agents. Like the assembly of a jigsaw puzzle, a relatively clear picture began to develop for about a dozen of the poisonings.

Filipina Narciso became an early suspect. Most of the poisonings occurred in the ICU, where Narciso worked. All but two of the suspected poisonings occurred during Narciso's shift and only on the days she was on duty. Later, it was determined that although the other two poisonings occurred on Saturday—not a regular workday for Narciso—she was on duty for those poisonings as well. When agents correlated the incidence of the poisonings with the work schedules of the entire hospital staff, only Narciso was on duty in the hospital during every poisoning.

Narciso was also identified by one of the patients/victims, John McCrery, who was interviewed by the FBI two days after his poisoning. McCrery recalled that he had seen a nurse, known to him as "Pia," inject something into his IV tube minutes before he went into respiratory arrest. (Narciso's nickname was Pia.) It was necessary for the agents to be certain of McCrery's identification, so the agents had Leonora Perez (she was not yet a suspect) and Bonnie Weston come into the room on a pretense. McCrery did not identify either as the nurse he had seen. Then the agents had Narciso come into McCrery's room. As soon as she entered the room, McCrery's pulse elevated, causing his heart monitor to sound an alarm. When Narciso left the room, McCrery said, "That's the one." As compelling as McCrery's identification would have been, it was ultimately ruled inadmissible. Two days after identifying Narciso, McCrery had heart bypass surgery. During the surgery, he went into cardiac arrest and almost died. Following the surgery, he was reinterviewed by the FBI, but his story changed dramatically, and based on known facts, it could not have been accurate. He was diagnosed as having suffered brain damage and died prior to trial. His identification of Narciso was ruled as inadmissible hearsay because he was not available for cross-examination.

Leonora Perez did not become a suspect until later in the investigation. A patient/victim, Richard Neely, told the agents he saw Perez inject something into his IV tube. To enhance Neely's recall, it was decided to hypnotize him. This was uncharted territory at the time and was possibly the first time hypnosis was used in an FBI case. Dr. Herbert Spiegel, a psychiatrist and hypnotist, was called in to place Neely in a trance. While under hypnosis, Neely seemed to recall the moments prior to his breathing failure more vividly. But Neely, like McCrery, died before the trial began.

In addition to Neely, a family member of Charles Gasmire, another victim, identified Perez as a suspect. On July 29, Richard Gasmire, the son of Charles, entered his father's room and saw a nurse near the head of his father's bed, doing something with the IV apparatus. She had her back to Richard and did not see him enter. He stood there for about two minutes. His father was sleeping when, suddenly, he sat up in bed and then collapsed. Charles Gasmire was going into Pavulon-induced respiratory failure. Richard Gasmire identified the nurse as Leonora Perez. To confirm his identification, the FBI set up a lineup of eighteen women wearing nurses' uniforms, fifteen of whom were Asian. Gasmire immediately identified Perez as the nurse he had seen in his father's room. Richard Gasmire did testify to what he had seen at the trial. After the initial response to the VAH poisoning and the need to interview hundreds of people, the investigation settled into the long process of building a case.

Two agents, Richard Guttler and Dan Russo, who had been involved in the case from the beginning, were assigned to continue the investigation to its conclusion. Guttler and Russo worked closely with two AUSAs, Richard Delonis and Richard Yanko.

In June 1976, a federal grand jury (FGJ) indicted Narciso and Perez. They were indicted on ten counts of poisoning, five counts of murder and one count of conspiracy to commit murder. (There was a superseding indictment in January 1977, but it did not substantially alter the charges.) The trial began in March 1977 and was one of the longest and most complex in the nation's history. It did not conclude until July 1977. The prosecution and verdict became a cause célèbre in Ann Arbor, across the nation and in the Philippines. It was widely believed that the nurses were made scapegoats, as they were immigrant Filipinos.

Ordinarily, a jury in a federal criminal trial can be picked in less than a day, but in this case, it took four weeks to pick sixteen jurors (this allowed for a jury of twelve with four alternates instead of the usual two because it was recognized that this would be an unusually long trial). At the conclusion of the trial, the sixteen jurors would be reduced, by lot, to twelve. (It was noted that the defense expressed great satisfaction with the jury that was selected.) In opening arguments, the government tried to prepare the jury by telling them it would be a long and complex case and that much of the case would be based on circumstantial evidence—no smoking guns or dripping syringes.

Much has been made about the fact that the government's case relied heavily on circumstantial evidence, as though that indicated the case was weak. But actually, circumstantial evidence is often more reliable than the recollection of witnesses. An example of circumstantial evidence that is often given is: "If you go to bed at night, and there is no snow on the ground, and you wake up in the morning and the ground is snow-covered, that is circumstantial evidence that it snowed during the night."

The prosecution had to prove in each of the charged poisonings that the victim had been illicitly administered Pavulon within three minutes of their respiratory arrest and that Narciso or Perez was in close enough proximity to have administered the Pavulon during the three-minute interval. Further, it would have to be shown there was no one else who could have injected the patient during the three-minute interval.

I have only outlined some of the prosecution's evidence, but over the course of the trial, the prosecution presented evidence of each of these elements, showing that only Narciso or Perez had been in the position to inject the Pavulon into the victims' IV tubes during the critical three-minute interval. (The government's case used eighty-nine witnesses, seventeen of whom were experts.) The prosecution never attempted to establish a motive for the poisonings, nor was that required, but it might have helped the prosecution if they could have explained why two hardworking, seemingly dedicated nurses would have gone on a poisoning spree. Any attempt to ascribe a motive to the nurses' acts would be speculative, but the most plausible explanation is that Narciso and Perez, like some other members of the VAH staff, thought the hospital was critically understaffed. Both Narciso and Perez made comments that indicated they were angry about the staff shortage at the hospital, and it was the belief of the prosecution that both women decided to dramatically demonstrate the need for more staff.

When the government rested its case, the lawyers for Narciso and Perez had to decide whether to present a defense or just argue that the prosecution had not proved their case beyond a reasonable doubt. The defense apparently believed that the prosecution's case was strong enough that they needed to not only present a defense, but they needed to put the defendants on the stand as well. This was a crucial turning point in the trial because it subjected their clients to cross-examination.

At the conclusion of the trial and after closing arguments, the case was given to the twelve jurors (eight women and four men). The jury deliberated for thirteen days, and by all accounts, they conscientiously and meticulously analyzed all the evidence that had been presented. At the beginning of the deliberation, some of the jurors believed that the two nurses were innocent, but as all the testimony was reviewed and compared, each juror became convinced that the nurses were guilty. The jury also concluded that because there were so many contradictions and inaccuracies in Narciso's and Perez's testimony, they were lying—repeatedly. (Several jurors were interviewed after the trial and spoke candidly about the deliberations and their conclusions.)

After the thirteen days of deliberation, the jury found both Filipino Narciso and Leonora Perez guilty of three counts of poisoning and conspiracy to poison patients. The jury did not find the nurses guilty on all of the poisoning counts, and they acquitted Narciso on the one remaining murder count, indicating how carefully they weighed the evidence regarding each incident. (The trial judge had previously directed a judgment of acquittal on the murder count against Perez and several of the poisoning counts.)

The outrage of the supporters of Narciso and Perez did not subside with the verdicts. The case was extremely complex, and it would have been very difficult to follow all of the testimony and evidence presented at the trial unless you were in court the entire time. The news reports were also incomplete. Consequently, few people understood the prosecution's case or the devastating ramifications of the nurses' testimony in their defense.

After receiving the verdict, the trial judge, Philip Pratt, ordered that Narciso and Perez undergo a sixty-day psychological evaluation. At the conclusion of the evaluation, in response to a defense motion, Judge Pratt ordered a retrial (not an acquittal), and he seemed to acknowledge the defendants' supporters' outrage (misinformed as it may have been) when he wrote (quoting from another source): "The question is, not whether any actual wrong resulted…but whether [there was] created a condition from which the general public would suspect that the jury might be influenced to reach a verdict on the ground of bias or prejudice." Judge Pratt went on to list several acts by the prosecution that the defense claimed were prejudicial errors. The judge characterized them this way: "No single claim of error raised by the defendants is sufficient to require reversal. There is no dramatic moment of prosecutorial misconduct."

What Judge Pratt did find was a pattern of prosecutorial conduct that he believed, in total, resulted in misconduct that would be remedied by a retrial. In other words, in the course of preparing for and trying a very lengthy and complex trial, the prosecution committed several innocuous errors that, when viewed cumulatively, could have prejudiced the jury. (However, we know, based on some of the jurors' statements, that this was not the case.)

During the long period of the investigation and prosecution of this case, a new U.S. attorney, James Robinson, was appointed. Robinson decided not to retry the case. Apparently, he was aware of the politics of the case, as he said, in effect, the public perception was that the nurses were innocent, and therefore, it would not be in the best interest of the government to pursue a retrial. (There were also tactical considerations, such as the fact that the nurses would probably not testify in a second trial and they could only be retried on the counts for which they were convicted.)

So, that is where the case ended. As much as their supporters would like to believe otherwise, Narciso and Perez were convicted of poisoning patients and conspiracy to poison. Though the verdict was set aside, it cannot be said that the nurses were innocent or that they were falsely accused.

3
THE TELLTALE FINGERPRINTS

I was seated facing Michael Lee Sprague as I interviewed him. We were on the same side of the table. I have never liked having anything between me and the person I am interviewing; it is easier to observe body language, and it doesn't give the person who is being interviewed the psychological shield of having an object between them and me. I was transfixed by Sprague's eyes. He had just confessed to a double homicide, but his eyes revealed nothing. I knew the aphorism, "The eyes are the windows to the soul." Sprague's eyes were more like black holes—they did not reflect light, they absorbed it.

But how did Sprague come to be arrested and interviewed by the FBI?

The story really begins in Jackson, Tennessee. Sprague was a drifter when he met Thomas Menth on the road, and they decided to travel together. In December 1975, they were picked up by two gay professors from Bethel College, which is located near Jackson. They had all gone to stay in a room at the Holiday Inn, where Sprague and Menth overpowered the professors. They bound and gagged them, stabbed them multiple times and slit their throats. Their throats were not just slit—the professors were nearly decapitated. The professors were found nude, and autopsies revealed that the victims had had "homosexual intercourse." The existence or use of DNA evidence had not yet been discovered. (But now, in addition to the FBI's national repository of fingerprints, the bureau maintains a repository of DNA, the FBI Laboratory's Combined DNA Index System, or CODIS. Today, DNA has the potential to be a better investigative tool than fingerprints.)

The murder scene was extremely bloody. When Sprague and Menth left the room, one of them put their hands, covered with the victims' blood, on the wall near the light switch. This left impressions with several fingerprints from both hands. These prints were "identifiable," but there was a problem. At the time, there was a common myth, probably propagated by movies and TV, that a fingerprint found at a crime scene could be matched with someone if their fingerprints were on record. However, the reality was that fingerprints were classified using all ten fingers. The central repository for all fingerprint records in the United States was the FBI Identification Division in Washington, D.C. (In 1924, J. Edgar Hoover, the director of the then Bureau of Investigation, championed the establishment of a national repository for fingerprints. In effect, it also became a national repository for criminal records. In 1967, with the advent of computers, that repository became the basis for the National Crime Information Center, or NCIC.)

When a person was arrested, their inked prints were put on a fingerprint card, which had premarked spaces for each finger. At the identification division, the card was classified by fingerprint examiners using the Henry classification system. Each fingerprint is unique, like a snowflake, but all fingerprints have common characteristics, which are referred to using terms like loops, arches and whorls. Using these common features, along with their infinite variations, each fingerprint is classified using numbers and letters. These individual classifications are written in a sequence that is determined by the order of the fingerprints on the card. The total sequence of all ten fingers is the final classification. At the time, if an investigator were lucky enough to find an identifiable fingerprint at a crime scene—that is, one that was at least partially classifiable—they could compare the single print to the fingerprints of a known suspect. But if there were no suspects, none could be identified with a found fingerprint alone.

Today, each fingerprint is digitally classified by a computer. The fingerprints can be electronically transmitted to the FBI's Criminal Justice Information Services Division in Clarksburg, West Virginia (the new Identification Division). So, now, a single fingerprint obtained at a crime scene can be immediately sent to the CJISD and, within minutes, matched with any of the hundred of millions of prints that are on file. Real-life crime detection has now caught up to the movies. (The new system is named the Automatic Fingerprint Identification System, or AFIS.)

But in 1975, all ten fingerprints were still needed for identification. The Jackson, Tennessee police had six or seven identifiable prints from the wall, and because they were found together, their sequence was discernible—that is, right index finger was right next to the middle finger, et cetera. The latent prints—those found at the scene—were sent to the FBI. As luck or fate would have it, they were received by a dedicated fingerprint examiner named Thurman Williams. Williams did a partial classification of the latent prints. Using that partial classification, he was able to narrow the possibilities of matching fingerprint cards on file to several thousand. But this was all assuming the person who had left their fingerprints on the wall also had their fingerprints on file. Williams would set aside time each day to methodically go through the stacks of fingerprint cards that might have matched the prints from the murder scene. After examining thosuands of cards, Williams got a hit. The person who left the bloody fingerprints was Thomas Menth, a petty criminal who had been arrested before and had his prints on file.

A warrant charging Menth with murder was issued in Jackson. Menth had no reason to believe he was wanted. He had been involved in a double murder in a town he was just passing through. No one knew him in Jackson, so how could he be a suspect? But Menth was tracked to New Orleans, where he was arrested. Being the "honorable" criminal he was, Menth quickly gave up Michael Sprague as the other murderer.

A murder warrant and a federal UFAP warrant were issued for Sprague. Sprague's hometown was New Haven, Michigan, so leads were sent to the Detroit FBI office to locate and apprehend him. So, we contacted Sprague's family and explained his plight. Within a few weeks, Sprague's mother told us that he was back in Michigan and staying at a motel on the eastside of Detroit. We went to the motel and arrested Sprague. He didn't resist or question why he was being arrested. We took him back to the FBI office, and I tried to make him comfortable. I knew it was important to illicit a confession from him, as the case against him was not strong. It would be nice to say that my outstanding interview technique resulted in Sprague's confession, but the truth is I think he was ready to confess.

Sprague gave us a detailed account of how he and Menth had met the two professors and subsequently murdered them. Sprague first met Menth while hitchhiking in Georgia. In December 1975, they were in Jackson, Tennessee, staying at a Holiday Inn. (They were using a stolen credit card to pay for the room.) He and Menth were drinking in the Holiday Inn lounge when two other men began talking to them. Sprague and Menth surmised that they were gay. The men said they were professors at a local college and invited them to go to another bar, where the professors paid for all the drinks. After a couple of hours, the professors drove Menth and Sprague back to the

Holiday Inn. Sprague said he was drunk when he went to their room. The professors and Menth followed Sprague to the room.

When they got into the room, Menth pulled out his .22-caliber short-barreled revolver, and then Sprague produced his .22-caliber derringer. Menth ordered both men to lie on the bed. After they bound and gagged the two men using electrical cords, Menth became agitated. Menth kept saying something about his old man being a "fag" and that he hated "fags." He hit one of the men in the head with his gun and slapped both of them around. Sprague said he didn't have anything against homosexual people, saying they were just "easy prey." According to Sprague, he never had any intent to kill the men, only to rob them.

Menth took both men's wallets and was going through them when he said they would have to take care of them to avoid being caught. Menth took a filleting knife from his backpack and handed it to Sprague before telling him to stab them. Sprague walked over to the bed and stabbed the men. He remembered that the men were facing each other but said his memory was hazy and that he couldn't remember how many times he stabbed them or where. (Sprague did not say anything about slitting the men's throats, nor did he indicate that either he or Menth had sex with the men.) Menth then said they had to leave, and he took a towel and wiped down the room to remove any fingerprints. He then used the towel to open the door and threw it back in the room as they left. (They somehow neglected to wipe the bloody fingerprints from the wall—the telltale fingerprints that would be their undoing.) They then took the professors' car and drove it to a location near Little Rock, Arkansas, where they abandoned it.

When Sprague finished describing the murders and how he and Menth had fled from Jackson, my partner, Paul Lindsay (who was my training agent and legendary in the bureau as a great fugitive hunter), pulled me aside and told me he was going to call the Jackson authorities to advise them that Sprague was in custody and had confessed. I was going to wrap up the interview.

Sprague told me how, after abandoning the car, he and Menth began hitchhiking south, through Arkansas and Texas. Sprague began telling me about truck stops and some of their rides when I considered finishing the interview. I knew that when the interview was finished, we would lodge Sprague in the Wayne County Jail. He would then be arraigned in federal court and assigned an attorney before being ordered removed to Tennessee. Once he had an attorney, it was likely that no one would have an opportunity to interview him again. As I was thinking about how I wanted to make sure we got it right, I was looking at Sprague's expressionless eyes, and he said, "Then we killed the old man in Texas." I wanted to react calmly so he would think I knew what he was talking about. So, I said something like, "Yeah, tell me about the 'old man.'" (I knew nothing about a murder in Texas.)

Sprague proceeded to tell me about how he and Menth had been picked up near Sealy, Texas, by a man in a newer car. He described the man as a white male in his fifties. The man then took them to his apartment in Sealy. He told the pair that he owned several movie theaters, and Sprague believed the man was homosexual. At the man's apartment, Menth took a shower and Sprague took a bath. After his bath, Sprague walked out of the bathroom and saw the old man bound and gagged. Menth was ransacking the apartment, trying to find money. When Menth was satisfied that he had found all the money, he handed Sprague the filleting knife from his backpack. Menth told Sprague to stab the man. This time, Sprague refused, so Menth took the knife and said, "It's easy." Menth then "stabbed the old man in the back many times." Sprague and Menth then took the old man's car and fled the area. On Interstate 10, near Beaumont, Texas, they abandoned the car and walked to a truck stop. They then hitchhiked to New Orleans, where they split up, and Sprague claimed he had not seen Menth since.

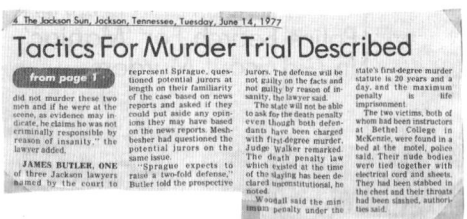

Newspaper coverage of the trial, with photographs of Michael Sprague (*left*) and Thomas Menth (*right*). *Courtesy of the* Jackson *(TN)* Sun.

I had Sprague give us a signed statement, and we contacted the police in Sealy to confirm that they had an unsolved murder matching the one described by Sprague. They also said they had neither suspects nor leads in the case. So, thanks to a Herculean effort by a fingerprint examiner, three murders were solved that probably would not have been resolved otherwise. I also believe Sprague and/or Menth would have continued to prey on gay men had they not been caught.

Epilogue

In June 1977, in Jackson, Tennessee, Sprague and Menth were both convicted of first-degree murder and received life sentences, the maximum they could receive. Both Paul Lindsay and I testified at the trial regarding Sprague's confession. At the time of their convictions, the U.S. Supreme Court had ruled that capital punishment was unconstitutional as it had been administered. Consequently, there was a moratorium in place on the imposition of the death penalty.

4
A DETROIT MOB PHOTOGRAPH BY THE FBI SURVEILLANCE SQUAD CAPTURES HISTORY

I joined the Detroit FBI surveillance squad in 1977. Two years later, on June 11, 1979, we witnessed an event—its historical significance and ramifications would not be clear until many years later.

But before I get to that, a little history. In the early 1970s, the FBI's Detroit Field Office established the FBI's first full-time surveillance squad. At that time, organized crime was one of the priorities of the FBI. Neil Welch, the then–Detroit FBI special agent in charge (SAC), decided it was a good idea to have a squad dedicated to following the members of the Detroit family of the LCN, the Mafia, and learning about their activities. It should be noted that the Detroit family was one of the oldest and most successful LCN families in the country. Although a surveillance squad was not a new concept, it was new for the FBI, and FBI headquarters had to be persuaded it was worthwhile. This meant the director at the time, J. Edgar Hoover, had to agree, and he did. The Detroit surveillance squad was born.

The squad was unique not just in its function but in its entire nature. As its primary target was a sophisticated organization that was surveillance wary, the squad had to be equal to the task. The agents who were assigned to the squad would no longer report to the FBI office but would work out of an "off-site" location that would use a phony business front. (It was later dubbed the bat cave.) The agents would not wear the usual agent garb of a coat and tie; instead, they would wear street clothes. The agents' cars would be various models and not have the staid four-door sedan look of a police car. Although radio communication between the agents' cars was a necessity, the radios and antennas had to be hidden.

The agents on the squad also had to learn techniques for conducting long-term surveillances undetected. They did not have the technological tools that are available today, such as GPS devices, laptop computers, cellphones and digitally coded radios. In those days, if you needed to have a phone conversation with someone when you were on the street, you had to find a payphone—of course, so did the bad guys. The agents also had to be adept at taking and developing photographs (there was no instant review, but the bat cave had a dark room). They had to learn the geography of the Detroit metropolitan area, and they had to be able to identify known members of the Detroit LCN family. In addition, they had to create and memorize code names for the family members and major streets because police radios were susceptible to being "scanned," or listened to by civilians. In fact, we learned through electronic surveillance that the Detroit family paid to have the FBI radio frequencies scanned regularly. (Today, FBI radios are digital and can be encrypted to National Security Agency [NSA] standards.)

Since the establishment of the Detroit FBI's surveillance squad, it has proven not only its usefulness in aiding the successful prosecution of the Detroit LCN but also its ability to provide information and evidence about criminal activities, including terrorism and foreign counterintelligence. The dedicated surveillance squad concept has been replicated in major field offices throughout the bureau.

And now, to that historic moment in 1979.

It was a beautiful summer day. We had set up to begin our surveillance that morning in Macomb County, north of Detroit, at a barber supply business owned by Rafaillo "Jimmy Q" Quassarano, a lieutenant in the Detroit LCN family. We had done surveillances there many times before and had no reason to believe that this day would be particularly notable. Later that morning, we saw Giacomo "Jack" Tocco, an upper-level LCN figure, arrive at the business. Then we saw Frank "the Bomb" Bommarito, a made man, arrive in a silver van. Bommarito went inside but, within minutes, exited and left driving another car. A few minutes later, Tocco and Quassarano exited the business with two other guys. They entered the van that Bommarito had brought and started driving west. We followed the van into rural Washtenaw County, to the Timberland Game Ranch (about fifty miles west of Detroit), which we later learned was owned by the Ruggirello brothers, Antonio "T.R." and Luigi "Louie the Bulldog," who were also made men in the Detroit family. The van entered the ranch, a large wooded area used for private upscale hunting excursions. We set up where we could observe the entrance to the ranch and saw several late-model Lincolns and Cadillacs, each with several occupants, drive into the ranch. (Later, when the gathering broke up, we had the Michigan State Police stop some of these cars to identify the occupants.)

None of us on the team had ever seen a meeting like this, and we were not sure what was happening. I decided that this was too big to not try to find out what was going on. So, another agent, Keith Cordes, and I went to the back of the ranch, away from the main gate. After scaling a fence (the statute of limitations on trespassing ran out a long time ago), we hiked through about a half mile of a heavily wooded area in the general direction of a part of the ranch that was cleared and contained some buildings. About one hundred yards from the cleared area, we could hear the voices of the men at the gathering. But we did not know if we could get much closer without being seen or heard, and we couldn't see much through the trees. Then I saw a narrow swath of cleared land radiating out from where the gathering was. It was an archery lane with a large target on our end. Keith and I got behind the archery target and we could see up the lane to where the family had gathered. Keith whispered to me, "Do you think it's a good idea to be this close to a target?" I replied, "I don't think mob guys do archery."

I had brought my camera with a 300-mm lens attached. Near the head of the lane, I could see three men standing together. Looking through my camera lens, I could see that it was Vito "Billy Jack" Giacalone and Anthony "the Bull" Corrado (both Giacalone and Corrado were capos, or captains, in the family) standing on either side of Jack Tocco. Resting my camera on the target, I snapped a photograph.

The surveillance team determined that almost everyone of any stature in the Detroit LCN family was at the game ranch that day, even some emeritus members—except for Anthony Zerilli. We also learned through source information that this meeting was called to make Jack Tocco the boss of the family, replacing Zerilli, whose performance had apparently been wanting. It is extremely rare for all of the members of a LCN family to meet. I was told by Scott Burnstein, a Mafia historian, that he knew of no other time when such a meeting of any LCN family had been witnessed by outsiders—not to mention photographed by them.

In March 1996, seventeen members of the Detroit family were federally indicted for violations of the RICO Act, conspiracy and related predicate crimes. Among those indicted were Vito Giacalone, Anthony Corrado and Jack Tocco. In January 1998, prior to the trial, Vito Giacalone pleaded

Above: The sign at the entrance to the wild game ranch. *Courtesy of the* Ann Arbor Observer.

Right: The surveillance photograph of Jack Tocco at the Detroit Mafia celebration of his promotion to boss of the family—Capos Vito Giacalone (*left*) and Anthony Corrado (*right*). *Author's collection.*

Jack Tocco booking photograph, 1997. *Scott Burnstein's collection.*

guilty, and in his plea statement in open court, he admitted there was a Detroit LCN family and that he was a member of it. This was the first time an upper-level member of the Detroit family had admitted its existence. A few months later, during the trial of Jack Tocco, Anthony Corrado and others, I testified about, among other things, the photograph I had taken almost twenty years before and the family gathering at the game farm. The photograph was admitted into evidence. (Jack Tocco died in 2014 of natural causes—the game ranch surveillance photograph survives on his Wikipedia page.)

At the trial, the United States presented evidence that had been gathered over a thirty-some-year period from informants, financial records, physical surveillance (FISUR) and court-authorized wire taps and microphone-electronic surveillance (ELSUR). In the end, Jack Tocco, Anthony Corrado and all but one of the others were convicted on fifty counts of racketeering (RICO), extortion and conspiracy.

Former assistant U.S. attorney Rick Convertino, one of the prosecutors in the trial, said of the 1979 photograph:

Tales of a G-Man

This page: Surveillance photograph of Anthony Corrado (1978) and booking photograph of Vito Giacalone. *Scott Burnstein's collection.*

The picture was extremely important. Obviously, it was important as information about the inauguration of Jack Tocco as head of the Detroit La Cosa Nostra. But the real key was that LCN members had never met all together at one time at a place that was not a wedding or a funeral. In hundreds and hundreds of hours of surveillance, nothing like that had ever happened before, and nothing like it ever happened again. All the planets were never lined up like that before or after that day.

But without the creation of a surveillance squad capable of conducting difficult surveillances and adapting to unique situations, that alignment of the planets would not have been witnessed or photographed.

5

KIDNAPPING FOR RANSOM

A Bad Business Model

It was February 1980 in Detroit. I was assigned to the FBI surveillance squad. It was very cold in the back of the van, as we had not yet installed a heater that would work when the van was not running. I had been driven to a spot where I could observe a ransom drop site from the small one-way window in the back of the panel van. The driver had parked the van and left. He was picked up a few blocks away by one of the other surveillance cars. If anyone was watching, they would think the van was empty.

This was one of the many kidnappings I would work in my career as an FBI agent. As I would witness, time and again, it was a lousy way for criminals to make money, particularly as technology improved. It became clear: the business model simply did not work, and I think it's worth recounting why.

In this 1980 case, my job was to watch the ransom package, which had been placed between the rear wall of a party store and a dumpster. The package contained $50,000. The "party store" (that is what they call convenience stores in Detroit) was at the corner of Fenkell and Robeson Streets on Detroit's northwest side. I had two HTs (handheld radios) with me in the van. One was tuned to the surveillance squad frequency, and the other was tuned to the frequency of the transmitter (tracking device) in the ransom package. The transmitter broadcast a rhythmic tone that would speed up if the package was moved—pretty primitive when compared to today's technology.

The whole thing started when Jacqueline Hempstead, the manager of a Detroit bank branch, learned that her son Hessley, age eight, had been kidnapped on his way to school. She was called by the kidnappers and received instructions and a ransom demand. Hempstead contacted her bank's security officer, who alerted the Detroit Police Department (DPD) and the FBI. It was decided that Hempstead would follow the kidnappers' instructions and comply with the ransom demand. A package with $50,000 and a transmitter was prepared. The FBI created a perimeter around the drop site. I had been driven to a spot near the drop site before the delivery; from there, I could observe the delivery and provide protection for Hempstead if necessary. Hempstead delivered the package without any problems. We had agents in the vicinity of the drop but none close enough to observe the package or spook someone who wanted to make a pickup.

After watching for several hours, I heard an ominous sound, a garbage truck approaching. The truck got in position and lifted the dumpster next to the ransom package. For a moment, I thought it was a novel way to retrieve a ransom. But when the dumpster was replaced, it was set on the top of the package. The transmitter screeched and then seemed to moan before dying completely. The package was torn open, with the stacks of bills clearly visible. I kept my vigil, but we were concerned that a passerby might see the cash. After about an hour with no apparent effort by the kidnappers to collect the ransom, we had Hempstead retrieve the package—or as much of it as she could.

In the meantime, young Hessley, who had been left unsupervised by the kidnappers at a house on Detroit's eastside, was able to break free and call home. Agents who were posted at the Hempstead home told him to get out of the house and go to a neighbor's house. He then went to the neighbors and called again. He was picked up by FBI agents and returned home. The kidnappers were initially identified from their connection to the house where Hessley had been held. They were successfully prosecuted. The kidnapping was short-circuited, but the victim was returned safely, and law enforcement responded quickly and performed well.

In 1975, my first year assigned to the Detroit division, there were four kidnappings in Michigan, three of which were classic kidnappings for ransom. The other was that of Jimmy Hoffa—a kidnapping/murder. It was an exciting first year on the job for me, but this was probably an inordinate number of ransom kidnappings for any city, including Detroit. Before I arrived, in much earlier times, it seemed as if criminals had far better luck with kidnapping. In Bryan Burroughs' book *Public Enemies: America's Greatest Crime Wave and the Birth of the FBI 1933–34*, he writes that for some of the notorious gangs of the era, kidnapping was the crime of choice. John

Dillinger's gang specialized in bank robbery, but the Barker-Karpis gang preferred kidnapping. It was the gangs' success in their respective specialty crimes that resulted in them becoming federal crimes, giving birth to the FBI. (Machine Gun Kelly, a member of the Barker gang, was credited with coining the "G-man" moniker for FBI agents when he was arrested by the FBI.) The FBI learned from those early experiences.

Kidnapping for ransom, out of necessity, requires a victim who comes from wealth or who has some access to wealth (part of the business model). Consequently, the victim will be or is often related, in some way, to a high-profile person who can be expected to have the wherewithal and desire to pay a ransom.

The federal statute that gave the FBI jurisdiction in kidnapping cases is called the Lindbergh Act, which arose from the highly publicized kidnapping of Charles and Anne Lindbergh's son by Bruno Richard Hauptmann and the proliferation of high-profile kidnappings elsewhere in the United States. Both of the Lindberghs were wealthy, but Charles may have been the most famous and beloved person in America at the time. The Lindbergh baby was found dead after a ransom was paid. It would be several years before the case was solved.

The federal kidnapping statute relies on a presumption that any kidnapping involves interstate commerce. It is a rebuttable presumption, but it allows the FBI to investigate a kidnapping without having to first establish some interstate aspect (18 USC §1201 et seq.).

One such case came with a kidnapping in Michigan on November 10, 1975. A young man, Timothy Stempel, age thirteen, was kidnapped in Bloomfield Township, an affluent suburb north of Detroit. Timothy's father was Robert Stempel, a high-ranking executive with General Motors (GM)—later, he would become the CEO of GM. Stempel received a series of phone calls at his home from the kidnappers, and he was told they wanted $150,000 for Timothy's return. Stempel contacted GM security, who, in turn, contacted the police and FBI.

Timothy had been kidnapped by two men, Darryl Wilson and Clinton Williams, who had decided that a good money-making project would be to kidnap a rich kid and hold him for ransom. They had no specific victim in mind when they drove to the high-income neighborhood of Bloomfield Township. They passed on a few potential victims for various reasons—playing too close to a house, too young, et cetera. Then they spotted Timothy. He was skateboarding. Williams asked Timothy for directions to a person's house. Timothy said he didn't know the person and started to walk away. Williams then pulled a handgun and

Front-page coverage of the Stempel kidnapping (1975). *Courtesy of the* Detroit Free Press.

told Timothy to get in the car. Timothy hit Williams with the skateboard, but Williams tackled him and struck him several times in the head. Williams and Wilson blindfolded Timothy and placed him in the backseat of the car. They drove to Wilson's apartment on the south side of Ann Arbor and transferred Timothy to the trunk of the car, where he remained for the next fifty hours. Williams then called Robert Stempel; he told him they had his son and that he would call back with instructions. Lastly, Williams told Stempel, "Don't tell the police."

The police and FBI committed hundreds of officers and agents to the investigation. It was designated "special" by FBI headquarters—all hands on deck. But it had to be done in such a way so as to not alert the kidnappers that the police were involved. The paramount goal in any kidnapping investigation is the safe return of the victim.

Robert Stempel received subsequent telephone calls on November 11 and again on the next day. Ultimately, he was instructed to go to an empty lot behind a roller skating rink in Inkster, a working-class suburb west of Detroit. He was to leave the money there, and he was told that he would be contacted about his son's release. The evening of the "drop," there was pouring rain. Efforts were made to surveil the ransom package, but because of the location and the weather, it was impossible without taking the chance of alerting the kidnappers. The package was retrieved, but whoever made the pickup was not seen. (Night vision equipment would have been helpful, but it was not yet available.)

Within a few hours, Timothy was released by the kidnappers not far from the drop site. Initially, there were no suspects, but because much of the activity had occurred in Inkster and nearby, "neighborhood" investigations were conducted. This included a canvassing of businesses and homes to determine if anyone had seen any relevant activity. At an apparel store, within a block of the roller rink drop site, an agent found that two men had spent several hundred dollars in cash on clothes. The serial numbers on the cash matched the numbers recorded from some of the ransom money, and the men who bought the clothes were identified. This is similar to how Bruno Richard Hauptmann was initially identified as the kidnapper of the Lindbergh baby. He had spent some of the ransom money, a gold certificate (few of those were still in circulation), at a gas station. The station attendant made a note of Hauptmann's license plate number. This is one of the reasons we now canvass neighborhoods.

The men aspiring to sartorial splendor were interviewed by FBI agents, and they explained how they had agreed to drive two men to the roller rink on the night of November 12 to retrieve a package containing money. The men assumed it was drug money and accepted several thousand dollars for their trouble. The men identified Darryl Wilson and said he lived in Ann Arbor, but they said they didn't know his address or the other man's name. The investigation determined that Wilson lived in an apartment on Ann Arbor's south side with a relative. A surveillance was set up at the apartment complex, and the car used in the kidnapping was found at the complex. Timothy Stempel, while locked in the trunk of the car, had carved his name on the inside of the trunk lid with a broken piece of a hacksaw blade he found in the trunk—pretty ingenious.

I was assigned to the surveillance. After a few hours, one of the other agents, Stan Lapekas, suggested we take a look in a dumpster at the apartment complex for possible evidence. The dumpster was inside a wood fence enclosure in the parking lot, and we could not be seen from the outside. After we had been in the enclosure for only a few minutes, a car drove in and parked right next to the enclosure gate. I peeked out and realized the driver was the subject, Darryl Wilson. As soon as he exited the car, Lapekas and I grabbed him and placed him in the backseat of our car, with us sitting very close on either side of him. We acted as if we already knew everything but wanted to give him an opportunity to tell his side of the story. After giving him his rights, he almost immediately confessed and gave up his accomplice, Clinton Williams. We had not had Williams's name until Wilson told us. Wilson also told us where Williams lived.

I got several other agents and drove to Williams's home to arrest him. Williams also confessed. He told us he had threatened Timothy Stempel with a handgun and hit him several times. He said they had kept Timothy in the trunk of a car for over two days. He also said that he had made the phone calls to Timothy's dad from a payphone in Inkster. (With the existing technology, we hadn't been able to trace the calls.) The subsequent search of Wilson's apartment resulted in the recovery of $137,000 of the ransom money.

The case and subsequent trial became a bit of a media circus. There was no interstate aspect of the kidnapping for it to be charged federally, so it was prosecuted in state court. The venue for the trial was Oakland County (Bloomfield Township), where the kidnapping occurred. The high-profile Oakland County prosecutor L. Brooks Patterson, who would later run unsuccessfully for governor, was the prosecutor. (He was later the Oakland County executive.) Even though the case was prosecuted in state court, most of the evidence would be provided by the FBI. So, an FBI agent, Tom Kelleher, was assigned to shepherd the case through prosecution.

Because of the media attention, the trial was moved from Oakland to Leland County in the northwest corner of Michigan's Lower Peninsula. On the first day of the trial, Patterson suspected that Wilson and Williams might have been planning to enter a plea. Patterson put Timothy Stempel on the stand and introduced the trunk lid as evidence. He then had me testify out of order to get Williams's confession on the record with all of the damning admissions. On the beginning of the second day of trial, Wilson and Williams entered guilty pleas with no plea bargain.

There were several other kidnappings for ransom in the Detroit division during my thirty-plus years there, but I am not aware of any that were successful. All of the kidnappers were identified and prosecuted. In two instances, although the ransoms were demanded and paid, the victims were murdered. In both those cases, the kidnappers never had any intention of releasing the victims alive.

The business model for kidnapping for ransom is flawed. It is a very high-risk crime. In some parts of the world, kidnappings are done with the collusion of the police—or at least their indifference—thus lowering the risk factor. The victim must fit a profile, and it is very difficult to successfully collect a ransom—probably more so today than in the technology-challenged period of my early career. Although the potential profits seem high, the odds of actually getting and keeping the ransom are extremely low.

In the latter years of my career, there were no kidnappings for ransom in Michigan. They also seem to be rare elsewhere in the country. I doubt that kidnapping for ransom is extinct in the United States, but it seems to be on the endangered list.

6

THE DOUBLE STEAL

Theft of Flat Glass Technology

In 1981, I was transferred to the Ann Arbor, Michigan Resident Agency (RA). For my first year in the RA, I was working foreign counterintelligence (FCI), and I was assigned a case involving the theft of technology—flat glass.

It took about five thousand years from the discovery of glass until a process was developed to economically mass produce flat glass, but it took only a few years for the technology to be stolen. Glass is one of the great fundamental inventions; it's not at the level of the wheel or fire, but it's pretty high on the list. Glass is chiefly made from relatively common and inexpensive raw materials: sand, soda ash (sodium carbonate) and lime. No one knows when glass was first invented or by whom. It does occur in nature when lightning strikes sand and sometimes during volcanic eruptions (obsidian). Its first use seems to have been as a glaze for ceramic vessels around 3,000 BCE. It was not until about 1,500 BCE that glass vessels were produced in Egypt (ultimately used to hold beer, one of my favorite inventions). The use of a pipe for blowing superheated glass was not invented until around 30 BCE.

Through the ages, uses for glass have multiplied and range from flat glass to optical lenses, which enabled the development of telescopes and microscopes. But this story is about the technology used to produce flat glass and why some people would go to great lengths to steal it.

Flat glass is used primarily for windows and doors on homes, buildings and vehicles. Until relatively recently, there was no economical way to produce large quantities of quality flat glass. Flat glass was originally made by blowing cylinders of glass that were then cut open, flattened and cut into panes. Most window glass, until the early 1800s, was made using the cylinder method. The cylinders were limited in size; they were six to eight feet (two to three meters) long and ten to fourteen inches (around thirty centimeters) in diameter, thus limiting the size of the panes that could be cut. Large windows had to be made using multiple panes.

In 1848, Henry Bessemer, an English engineer, designed a system that produced a continuous ribbon of flat glass by forming the ribbon of molten glass between rollers. This was an expensive process, as the surface of the glass had to be ground and polished, but it overcame the size limitations of the cylinder method. Beginning in the 1920s, continuous ribbons of glass would be passed through lengthy series of inline grinders and polishers, reducing glass loss and cost.

The ultimate breakthrough in the production of flat glass didn't come until the late 1950s, when Sir Alastair Pilkington and Kenneth Bickerstaff of Pilkington Brothers Ltd. in the United Kingdom developed the first successful commercial float glass process. The float glass process uses common raw materials for glass production. The materials are mixed with cullet (waste glass) in a furnace where it is heated to around 2,800 degrees Fahrenheit (1,500 degrees Celcius). When the mixture becomes molten, it is poured onto a "tin bath," a bath of molten tin about 2.3 inches (6 centimeters) deep, 3 to 4 feet (3 to 4 meters) wide and 150 feet (45 meters) long. The glass then enters a canal; the speed and volume of the glass flow is controlled by a gate called a twill. The glass literally floats on top of the tin with uniform thickness. (The molten tin does not adhere to the glass, but an oxygen-free atmosphere must be maintained to keep the tin from oxidizing and adhering to the glass.) As the glass flows along the tin bath, the temperature is gradually reduced. At the end of the bath, the glass has cooled to approximately 1,100 degrees Fahrenheit (600 degrees Celcius). At that temperature, the glass can be lifted from the bath and put onto rollers. The glass ribbon is then pulled by the rollers at a controlled speed. The speed at which the glass is pulled determines its thickness. As the glass is pulled from the bath, it passes through a lehr (a type of kiln), where it gradually cools so that it anneals and does not crack from a more rapid temperature change. After exiting the lehr, the glass is cut by machines.

Pilkington Bros. patented the process to protect the substantial cost of development and have a competitive advantage. Virtually all flat glass is now made using the float glass process, including the glass for car windshields and windows.

Since the time of Henry Ford, Ford Motor Co. has embraced the industrial strategy of vertical integration. That is, not only building cars but also producing the raw materials and many of the car's components. This included the glass and fabrication of the windshields and windows. Ford realized that the float glass process was not only more efficient, but it also produced superior flat glass with consistently better visibility—an essential characteristic for windshields. Consequently, Ford negotiated with Pilkington Bros. and obtained the licensing rights to manufacture glass using the float process. Ford built a float glass plant at their Rouge complex. (Located on the Rouge River, just west of Detroit, the Rouge complex was, at one time, the largest industrial complex in the world.)

In 1932, Guardian Glass Co. was originally established as a small fabricator of windshields in Michigan. William "Bill" Davidson, a nephew of the company's owner, became the chief executive officer (CEO) in 1957, just ten years after graduating from the University of Michigan. (The late Bill Davidson might be more well known as the owner of the Detroit Pistons during their heyday as NBA champions. Those teams were known as the "Bad Boys.") Davidson had Guardian declare bankruptcy and reorganized the company under chapter 11.

After three years with Davidson at the helm, Guardian came out of bankruptcy but continued to struggle.

Although Guardian had obtained the contract for all American Motors windshields, it was clear that to be more profitable, it would have to produce its own glass. It had been buying the glass it used from glass producers, primarily Ford. The U.S. glass industry was dominated by an oligarchy of three companies: Pittsburgh Plate Glass (PPG), Libbey Owens Ford and Ford. Davidson concluded that Guardian needed to be a glass producer.

Davidson was set to carry out an audacious plan. He hired away Ford's chief glass engineer, Ed Sczesny, and began planning to build a float glass plant in Carlton, Michigan. Clearly, Sczesny brought proprietary technology and trade secret information with him. Guardian made a perfunctory request of Pilkington to obtain licensing rights, which Pilkington denied. Pilkington threatened to sue if Guardian moved forward with the float plant. Davidson gambled that Pilkington would not sue, as it risked jeopardizing its entire worldwide licensing program if it sued Guardian and lost.

Construction on the float plant began in 1969 and was completed at a cost of about $17 million. By the middle of 1970, the plant was producing 350 tons of glass per day. Guardian reached an ongoing royalty agreement with Pilkington in 1971 but at substantially lower rates than the other U.S. licensees paid. The lower payments were based on Pilkington not providing any technical assistance to Guardian. (This must have been troubling to Ford, which was paying the higher licensing fees and had lost its chief glass engineer.)

The gamble had paid off. Today, Guardian is one of the four largest flat glass manufactures in the world. It has eighteen thousand employees with plants in twenty-one countries. Davidson became a billionaire and a philanthropist. He donated millions of dollars to different causes and institutions; among them was the University of Michigan, to which he donated $55 million.

A Turkish-American engineer who was working for Ford as glass engineer, John Akfirat, was aware of what Davidson and Sczesny had done. In 1973, Akfirat stole the blueprints for the Ford float glass plant. Ford discovered that Akfirat was trying to sell their plans and his expertise and notified the FBI. The FBI used an undercover agent posing as a potential buyer to approach Akfirat. The plans were seized, and Akfirat was arrested and prosecuted. Akfirat pleaded guilty and served a short jail sentence.

In the 1980s, a foreign source reported that a float glass plant was being built in Romania (this was during the Cold War, and Romania was part of the Soviet Bloc.) The source also reported that Akfirat was involved in the construction of the plant. Akfirat had been traveling to Romania from his home in Ann Arbor, Michigan, during the period when the plant was being constructed, between 1975 and 1981. The U.S. attorney in Michigan decided that a criminal investigation should be initiated, and the FBI was able to obtain the plans for the Romanian plant.

Prior to working this case, I did not have a clue how flat glass was made. It was imperative that I learn in order to conduct interviews and understand what had been stolen. As part of the investigation, I took the plans for the Romanian plant to Pilkington Bros. in Saint Helens, United Kingdom (near Liverpool). Pilkington engineers determined that there were several unique characteristics in the Romanian plans, which proved they had used patented and/or secret technology to build the plant.

Akfirat was prosecuted and pleaded guilty again, in this case, to one count of wire fraud. He was cooperative; a mitigating factor may have been that the Romanian plant was never successful, or maybe the judge understood that Akfirat was just trying to execute a double steal, a play in baseball in which two base runners each steal a base at the same time. He was sentenced to probation.

Akfirat was federally charged with wire fraud because, at the time, there were no federal statutes that specifically addressed the theft of "trade secrets." In 1996, federal statutes were enacted, outlawing economic espionage and the theft of trade secrets (18 USC §1831, §1832). I am not aware that criminal prosecution was ever contemplated for Davidson and Sczesny's theft of trade secrets, but had these laws been on the books, they could have been prosecuted.

7

THE ANNUAL TALK WITH THE MICHIGAN FOOTBALL TEAM ABOUT SPORTS GAMBLING

> *Louis, I think this is the beginning of a beautiful friendship.*
> —*Rick Blaine (Humphrey Bogart) to Captain Louis Renault (Claude Rains) in the closing line of* Casablanca

In 1982, legendary Michigan football coach Bo Schembechler asked the Ann Arbor FBI office to talk to his team about the perils of illegal sports gambling. The senior resident agent at the time, Tom Love, agreed to make the presentation. Love, knowing that I had played college football at Nebraska (read: mostly practiced), asked me to help with the presentation. We explained that sports gambling is not about who wins but about covering the point spread. Gamblers and bookies need to get inside information as an edge to better divine how a team will perform. They are on the lookout for sources, like players or trainers, who can provide that inside information. The Holy Grail for gamblers and bookies would be to get a cooperating player or referee with the ability to control the point spread—"point shaving."

Sports gambling was and is a potential threat to the integrity of sports. The huge amount of money bet illegally in the United States, estimated at more than $300 billion, is an incentive to control the outcome of a game. (When we were doing the presentations, it was illegal under federal law for states to authorize sports gambling, except where it existed prior to the law. However, that law was overturned by the U.S. Supreme Court in 2018. States can now authorize sports gambling, and in the states where it has been authorized, it has proliferated, especially on the internet. There are still illegal sports gambling operations, and legal and illegal sports gambling continues to be a threat to the integrity of sports.)

When we started making presentations, Michigan's football team was housed in a relatively small one-story building. Michigan's transition to the state-of-the-art facilities it has today is emblematic of the change in Division 1 football in the past thirty years. In the early days, college teams like Michigan might be on TV once or twice a year. Now, a dedicated fan or gambler can watch just about any game played anywhere in the country. This has resulted in a tremendous increase in revenue for Division 1 intercollegiate sports. Also, with the increase in TV coverage, sports gambling has increased. And with the advent of the internet, gamblers have access to more current information and can place bets online.

The FBI recognized the need for educating players early on and developed a sports presentation program. I went through the training and attended periodic conferences with representatives from the NFL, MLB, NBA, NHL and NCAA. Over the years, I have talked to professional and collegiate teams.

We talked to the Michigan basketball teams several times, including the "Fab Five" teams. That might have been a case of a failure to communicate in the case of some players. In a subsequent investigation, we found out that a man, Eddie Martin, was running a large "numbers racket," an illegal lottery, and was paying some of the Michigan basketball players, a violation of NCAA rules. Since he ran a large "numbers game," we suspected he was a sports gambler and was trying to fix games. As it turned out, he was just a Michigan "booster" who wanted to encourage highly recruited players to play for Michigan. One of the Fab Five players was Juwan Howard. Howard was not involved with the Eddie Martin's payments to players and was one of the few Michigan basketball players who thanked us for our presentations. After a successful career in the NBA, Howard is now Michigan's head basketball coach. Warde Manuel, the Michigan athletic director, who hired Howard, was a Michigan football player on some of Bo's teams. Warde also thanked us for our talks—nice to know those guys were listening.

Bo Schembechler invited us back the next year, and Love asked me to give the presentations on my own. Over the years, I would bring other FBI agents to help with the presentations: Marty Torgler, Lou Fischetti, Jim Brennan and Hugh Shanahan from the DEA, who did a very entertaining talk about illegal drugs. Little did I know that it was to be the "beginning of a beautiful friendship" between Bo and me—one that would have a substantial effect on my career.

Michigan football coach Glenn "Bo" Schembechler with the author. *Author's collection.*

Bo had a concept of a "Michigan Man," a student-athlete who not only demonstrated traditional values, such as integrity, honor and responsibility on the field, but they lived them as well. He and I worked together on several FBI cases—notably, the investigation of Norby Walters and Lloyd Bloom, two notorious sports agents who bribed and signed about twenty blue-chip college football players while they were still eligible to play college ball. Walters and Bloom postdated the contracts and kept them secret, a clear violation of NCAA rules. Under those rules, once a player signs with an agent, his college eligibility ends. Bo was the "star" witness in the successful federal prosecution of Walters and Bloom. Walters had organized crime connections, and it was believed that the ultimate goal of signing so many star athletes was to get some of the players involved in point shaving.

Bo also convinced me to pursue an undercover operation targeting the illegal trafficking of anabolic steroids. That operation, called Equine, was international in scope and resulted in the successful prosecution of more than seventy dealers. We also learned that many major-league baseball players were using steroids. Ironically, I first warned the MLB about the steroid problem in 1994 at an FBI sports presentation conference (chapter 16).

Although illegal sports gambling continued to be the primary topic of our presentations, over the years, other concerns were discussed, such as drugs, steroids, domestic violence and, more recently, the improvident use of social media.

Something I didn't always do but later learned was important was to ensure that the head coaches stayed during the presentations because if the coaches didn't think it was important to be there, the players wouldn't either.

After Bo retired in 1989, I continued to talk to the Michigan football teams. Later, I was fortunate to become friends with Lloyd Carr during his thirteen-year tenure as Michigan's coach. Carr coached my son, Andy, when he was a walk-on from 2000 to 2003. Those presentations were special for me, as I was not only an FBI agent speaking to Michigan's football team, but also a father seeing his son in a group of men representing a program that I had come to respect.

There were some outstanding men and players (numerous All-Americans and two Heisman Trophy winners) in those audiences. Many would go on to careers in the professional leagues, but most would have successful careers in all walks of life. It was a great opportunity to project a positive image of the FBI.

I retired in 2006, but I continued to talk to the Michigan football teams until 2014. The topics changed, but the overall message stayed the same: make good choices based on good values. I always ended my talks with a quote attributed to John Wayne: "Life is tough. It's tougher if you're stupid."

8
PRINT THE FACT

How the Unabomber Was First Identified

There is a memorable scene near the end of the classic John Ford movie *The Man Who Shot Liberty Valance*, a parable about the triumph of the rule of law in the Old West. In one of the last scenes, the editor of the local newspaper has just heard the true story of the killing of Liberty Valance, an extremely bad guy and notorious gunfighter, from Jimmy Stewart's character, Ranse Stoddard. Stoddard is in the autumn of an extremely successful political career that began, at least in part, because he had been proclaimed a hero for having killed Valance. But as Stoddard explains to the editor, he did not kill Liberty Valance. When the interview with Stoddard ends, a young reporter asks the editor if he's going to use the story. The editor replies, "This is the West. When the legend becomes fact, print the legend."

Several years ago, I had a Liberty Valance moment when I was out to dinner with my wife. A local judge who I have known for years walked up to our table and introduced me to his wife as the FBI agent who identified the Unabomber. I sort of demurred and said something like, "I helped, but it was a team effort." This was not the first time I have been given credit for identifying the Unabomber, and although it is technically true, it's definitely misleading. So, here is the story:

I first became involved in the UNABOM investigation because one his bombs had been sent to Ann Arbor. ("UNABOM" was bureau shorthand for "university and airlines bomber," and it was used as the title of the case. And yes, the second "b" was dropped in the bureau spelling.) In November

1985, a package weighing about five pounds and measuring three by eight by eleven inches was received in the mail at the residence of Professor James McConnell. At the time, McConnell was teaching and conducting research in the psychology department at the University of Michigan. McConnell had done research and considerable writing on behavior modification in the 1950s and early 1960s and had gained some national notoriety. (Later, we came to understand that McConnell had been targeted because of his research and being a proponent of behavior modification, something Kaczynski, or the Unabomber, was vehemently opposed to.) The package was opened by an assistant of McConnell. It exploded and caused considerable damage to McConnell's kitchen, but the assistant only suffered minor injuries to his arms and abdomen.

This was the tenth bomb in a series of sixteen sent by the Unabomber between 1978 and 1995. The bomb had been secreted in a hole cut in a ream of paper. The explosive device was basically a pipe bomb filled with ammonium nitrate and aluminum powder. The pipe was sealed at both ends by wooden caps, rather than the usual threaded metal caps. The igniter was a nail held in tension by rubber bands, poised to strike multiple match heads when disturbed by someone opening the package. Because of this rudimentary construction, the bomb did not explode with anything near its potential power. Later bombs were more efficient and resulted in the deaths of three people and severe injuries to others.

One of the maddening elements of the Unabomber investigation was that there did not seem to be a common thread connecting the recipients of the bombs. And the construction of the bombs, although similar, was done with components that proved to be untraceable. It wasn't until the Unabomber's convoluted manifesto was published that some overarching motive could be discerned.

When Attorney General Janet Reno and FBI Director Louie Freeh persuaded the reluctant editors of the *New York Times* and *Washington Post* to publish the manifesto in its entirety—thirty-five thousand words—it was hoped that someone would read it and associate it with the person who was the Unabomber. It is a testament to Ted Kaczynski's isolation that only one person, Ted's estranged brother, David Kaczynski, could identify him. But had it not been for Ted's hubris in demanding his manifesto be published, he may never have been identified.

David's wife, Linda, saw some common themes between the manifesto and some of Ted's professed philosophy, but neither she nor David had had any contact with Ted for years. She encouraged David to read the manifesto. (Linda had thought Ted might be the Unabomber for some time prior to the publication of the manifesto.) David was struck by the similarity between some of the ideas and phrases in the manifesto and some old letters and essays that Ted had written him. In the writings, Ted had expounded on his antitechnology philosophy.

In the fall of 1995, David and Linda contacted a friend, Susan Swanson, who was an attorney/investigator, regarding their concerns about David's brother. Swanson contacted Clinton Van Zandt, a retired FBI agent. Van Zandt, a hostage negotiator for the FBI, had been assigned to the FBI's Behavioral Analysis Unit, which, among other things, does criminal profiling. Swanson took the letters, from which almost all the names and identifying information had been removed, to Van Zandt and asked him to determine whether or not the author of the letters was the author of the manifesto. After reviewing the material, Van Zandt concluded that there was about a 50 percent chance that the authors of the letters and the manifesto were the same. Van Zandt was not impressed enough with any similarity to pursue the information further. Swanson had been investigating this matter pro bono but was unable to continue.

Ted Kaczynski's photograph that was attached to his application to the graduate school of the University of Michigan. *Author's collection.*

The Kaczynskis' concerns had not been alleviated, so they contacted another attorney they knew who was practicing in Washington, D.C., Anthony Bisceglie. Bisceglie knew FBI agent Mike Harrison assigned to the Washington Field Office (WFO) and apprised him of David and Linda's concerns without identifying them. He also provided Harrison with some of the redacted documents. Harrison believed there was sufficient similarity in the writings to justify passing them on to another agent in WFO, Molly Flynn, who was handling UNABOM leads. Flynn also believed there were significant similarities in the documents and the manifesto. She contacted the Unabom Task Force (UTF) in San Francisco and told them about the redacted letters and their similarity to the manifesto. All of the documents were transmitted to the UTF. Fortunately, in the documents, some hints were mistakenly not redacted: the name "Ted" appeared, and there were references to Harvard, University of Michigan and the University of

California in Berkeley. (Bisceglie was not aware of the tell-tale information that remained in the documents.)

The UTF, which was composed of FBI agents, postal inspectors and Bureau of Alcohol, Tobacco and Firearms agents, had been coordinating the UNABOM investigation and had recently been inundated with tips as a result of the publishing of the manifesto. None of these tips was of any value, but they had to be investigated nonetheless. The information Flynn provided stood out and seemed to have some promise. Several UTF agents investigated the information to identify the author. Joel Moss, an FBI supervisor assigned to the UTF, pursued the possible Michigan connection.

On the evening of February 12, I was working late when I received a call from Joel. I knew Joel, as we had talked in the past about the UNABOM investigation and the McConnell bombing. He explained the letters, the manifesto and some information that might be useful in identifying the author to me. They had determined that his name was Ted (a derivation of either Theodore or Edward), he had been born in the Chicago area, he had done undergrad study at Harvard (probably in mathematics) and thereafter obtained or sought a PhD at the University of Michigan (UM) between 1968 and 1972. It was believed that subsequent to being at Michigan, Ted taught mathematics at the University of California at Berkeley (UC Berkeley). The UTF was making inquiries at UC Berkeley, but as of yet, they had not been successful. Joel impressed upon me the sensitivity of the information and said that it had to be handled as expeditiously as possible. In other words, I needed to quickly get personal information from the University of Michigan regarding a possible PhD candidate whose name I did not know, and I could not tell them why I was asking.

Kaczynski (*left*), following his arrest at a court appearance. A sketch of the Unabomber based on a witness's description. *Author's collection.*

I had been in Ann Arbor and around the university long enough to know that the people there would not welcome the FBI with open arms, nor would I have any control over how many people became aware of the investigation. Further, they would refuse to do anything without a subpoena, and nothing would happen quickly. But I had a friend, Jim Smiley, the assistant director of the UM Department of Public Safety and the UM Police. He was a graduate of the FBI National Academy (the prestigious school for law enforcement executives taught by the FBI at Quantico), and we had worked together on many occasions. I called Jim and told him I needed to identify an individual who may have received a PhD from UM but that I didn't know his full name, et cetera. I did not tell him that the guy might be the Unabomber; I just said it was extremely important and extremely sensitive. Jim did not question my sanity, nor did he say such a check couldn't be done without more information. Instead, he said that he would see what he could do. Within a few hours, Jim called me back and told me that he had come up with five possible names, but only one seemed to fit all the criteria: Theodore Kaczynski. To Jim's credit, he never asked me what the inquiry was about.

I immediately called Joel Moss and gave him the name Theodore Kaczynski and what background information UM had about him. Joel told me that I was to tell no one else. "At this moment, there are only two people who know the identity of the Unabomber."

It is my understanding that within a few days, the UTF was contacted directly by Anthony Bisceglie. Initially, Bisceglie had some preconditions that he wanted to be agreed to before disclosing the identity of the Unabomber. Joel Moss and others on the UTF explained to the attorney that perhaps the discussion could move more quickly if the attorney knew that the UTF already had the name Ted Kaczynski.

Over the next few weeks, while the FBI had Kaczynski under surveillance in Lincoln, Montana, and search warrants were being prepared, I was making discreet inquiries regarding Ted's time at UM. I learned that he was a brilliant, if eccentric and socially inept, student who had studied theoretical mathematics.

About six weeks later, when Ted was arrested and the little cabin where he was living was searched, considerable evidence was found linking him to the bombings, including a live bomb that was ready to be sent. Joel Moss sent me a copy of Ted's handwritten diary that was found at the cabin. I was particularly interested in what he had written about his time at UM: "These were the most miserable years of my life." However, Ted did not send the bomb to Professor McConnell because he was a disgruntled

Michigan student; he sent it because he hated psychologists who were doing behavioral modification research.

Although brilliant, Ted had many demons. He viewed himself as intellectually superior to other students and faculty. He first contemplated killing people while he was a student at Michigan:

> *What was entirely new was the fact that I really felt I could kill someone. My first thought was to kill somebody I hated and then kill myself before the cops could get me. (I've always considered death preferable to long imprisonment.) But, since I now had new hope, I was not ready to relinquish life so easily. So, I thought, I will kill, but I will make at least some effort to avoid detection, so that I can kill again.*

Ted Kaczynski is currently serving a life sentence—"long imprisonment"—with no possibility of parole at the federal penitentiary in Florence, Colorado, the "Super Max," where he is locked down for twenty-three hours a day.

So, technically, I identified the Unabomber, but in reality, I was merely a cog in the machinery that was already moving inexorably toward knowing that Ted Kaczynski was the Unabomber.

Print the fact not the legend.

9

THE FBI GETS JURISDICTION TO INVESTIGATE DRUG TRAFFICKING

Webster Bivens may have been a drug dealer, but his place in law enforcement history is not proportional to his status as an alleged dealer.

In the fall of 1965, Federal Bureau of Narcotics (FBN) agents raided Bivens's Brooklyn apartment. The FBN agents had neither an arrest warrant nor a search warrant. The agents arrested Bivens and handcuffed him in front of his family. They also allegedly threatened his family and, in the terminology of Bivens's later lawsuit, searched his apartment from "stem to stern." No drugs were found, and the charges that were filed after Bivens's arrest were dismissed.

Bivens apparently had a litigious streak and brought a civil action against the "six unknown agents" of the FBN based on the violation of his rights under the Fourth Amendment: "The right of the people to be secure in their persons, houses, papers and effects against unreasonable searches and seizures, shall not be violated, and no warrants shall issue, but upon probable cause, supported by oath or affirmation, and particularly describing the place to be searched, and the person or things to be seized."

Until that time, a cause of action could not be brought against the United States or its agents unless it was specifically authorized under certain statutes, and that was the ruling of the lower courts in Bivens's action. But the Bivenses case made it to the U.S. Supreme Court, and in 1971, the court decided that the United States could be sued if the acts of its agents violated the Constitutional rights of an individual. This not only created a cause of action, but it also fostered a perception that federal drug agents were running amok and were incapable of doing more than simple "buy-bust" investigations.

As the Bivens case worked its way through the courts, the whole approach to the federal war on drugs was being evaluated. The FBN agents who arrested Bivens were part of the Department of the Treasury, presumably because drugs, like alcohol, were viewed as taxable commodities, even though the principal drugs being targeted at that time were heroin, cocaine and marijuana—all illegal and not taxable.

To unify the federal effort against illegal drugs, one agency was created in 1968: the Bureau of Narcotics and Dangerous Drugs (BNDD). It was to be an investigative agency in the Department of Justice. Then, in 1973, the BNDD was renamed the Drug Enforcement Administration (DEA), and it remained in the DOJ. Although the perception of drug agents out of control was mostly inaccurate, the DEA did have limited resources and was under pressure to produce results in terms of arrests and drug seizures. This made it difficult for the agency to dedicate its limited resources to long-term investigations targeting the upper echelons of drug trafficking organizations.

In the meantime, the FBI was learning to utilize the tools provided by the Omnibus Crime Act of 1968. This lengthy act was intended to provide means for federal law enforcement to investigate organized crime. For the FBI, that meant investigating La Costa Nostra, the Mafia. One particular part of the act (title III) prescribed the process to legally intercept wire, oral or electronic communications—electronic surveillance or "ELSUR" for short. It included telephone wiretaps and surreptitiously placed microphones or bugs—generally referred to as a "wire." The probable cause required to get judicial approval for ELSUR was, by design, a difficult standard to meet. The affidavit documenting this "special" probable cause often ran well in excess of one hundred pages. Among other things, there had to be proof that other investigative techniques would not work. For example, if a drug dealer would only deal with someone he has known for years, it would be extremely difficult to get him to deal with an undercover agent. Once the affidavit and accompanying order are written, they must be submitted to the attorney general of the United States or a specifically designated assistant attorney general for approval. If they are approved, they must be authorized by a U.S. District Court judge in the district where the ELSUR is to be conducted. The ELSURs are limited to thirty days but can be renewed based on an updated affidavit.

In 1982, the FBI was given collateral jurisdiction with the DEA to conduct drug investigations. Until then, the FBI had no drug jurisdiction. One of the primary reasons for giving the FBI drug jurisdiction was that the FBI had demonstrated success in investigating organized crime, like the Mafia, using ELSUR and other techniques. The FBI hit the ground running. Soon after getting drug jurisdiction, there were numerous drug cases initiated by the FBI. The FBI not only had an advantage with the techniques it had mastered, but it also had a physical presence all over the United States not just in major urban areas. Because of that presence, the FBI had developed a strong working relationship with local law enforcement.

What the FBI did not have was an intelligence base. Who were the possible drug dealers, and how were their organizations structured and operated? That intelligence could, to some extent, be provided by the local law enforcement. A symbiotic relationship developed, as local police intelligence could be used to develop sufficient probable cause for ELSUR. In Michigan, the police didn't have any authority to intercept oral or telephonic communications, but the federal agents could provide that. The FBI also integrated the IRS and the DEA into these investigations.

In Michigan in early 1982, there were several drug investigations initiated by the FBI, working with local police. Based on source information, the work of undercover police officers and federal agents and physical surveillance, probable cause was developed to pursue ELSUR coverage, targeting upper-echelon drug dealers. Many of the drug organizations were connected with other organizations. Investigations in Flint and Saginaw led to information about a large marijuana distribution operation in Ann Arbor. That operation turned out to be even larger than we thought. Ultimately, all of the members of the organization were prosecuted. The leaders were brothers Ned and Fred Shure, who the media dubbed the "Barons of Pot." Ned Shure, a successful businessman before he became involved in the marijuana business, and Fred Shure, a professor of nuclear physics at the University of Michigan, made millions, tax free, from the sale of literally semitruck loads of pot. The Shure brothers eschewed the distribution of drugs other than marijuana, but not everyone in their organization did.

In Ann Arbor, the FBI had gone up on a wiretap and bug of Albert Papson Jr., a subdealer of the Shures. That led to overhearing a conversation between Papson and James Tanceusz. Tanceusz had stopped by Papson's home, and he and Papson discussed Papson buying eight ounces of cocaine from Tanceusz. The visit and conversation were a surprise. When the conversation was overheard, we didn't know who Papson was talking to.

Fortunately, there was a physical surveillance of Papson's home at the time of Tanceusz's visit. The surveillance team was able to identify Tansceusz and follow him home. Based on that encounter, an investigation of Tansceusz was begun and assigned to me.

The Ann Arbor Police Department's Special Investigations Unit had been tracking Tansceusz and his associates since late 1978 through surveillance, debriefing confidential informants and reviewing business, financial and telephone records. However, they were unable to infiltrate the organization or gather enough conspiratorial evidence to justify prosecution (from my Tanceusz affidavit).

James Gregory Tanceusz (rhymes with Kansas) was an interesting character. He had graduated from the University of Michigan and had been on the Michigan football team in 1969, when Bo Schembechler arrived. Bo was a daunting taskmaster and laid down the challenge that those who stayed would be champions. Tansceusz did not stay.

Part of the expertise necessary in conducting investigations using wiretaps and bugs is the actual installation of the devices. The FBI had established a relationship with the telephone company (in those days, there was only one); it was required, by law, to cooperate, and the government compensated it for its services. The FBI had agents who had been trained to install wiretaps, and these "technical" or "tech" agents worked with certain telephone employees who were sworn to secrecy. The tech agents were also trained to conduct surreptitious entries—burglaries—in order to place the bugs. These entries were requested in the ELSUR affidavits and were authorized by U.S. District Court judges. The entries had to be carefully choreographed to avoid detection, ideally when no one was there. Usually, the occupants were surveilled after they left to make sure they didn't unexpectedly return while the tech agents were inside. The tech agents would do a survey of the target residence or business before making their entry. This would give them an opportunity to determine the best place to make an entry, what type of lock(s) had to be compromised, whether there were dogs and/or alarms, et cetera. All of this had to be done in such a way that the subject drug dealer would not be aware that the entry had occurred.

With Tanceusz's residence, some of these issues were easy to resolve. His house was in the country, so there were no neighbors nearby. He didn't have a dog or an alarm system. The house was a single-story ranch house. The bug was placed in the living room. It was sensitive enough to pick up conversations in other parts of the house. This was both a benefit and a problem. If Tanceusz played music or had the TV on, it would tend to drown out the conversations. (There were ways to filter out the extraneous noise, but they were not completely successful.)

For the bug, the tech agents installed a separate phone line. The bug, in effect, was an open phone line. An observant person might have noticed an extra line running from the house to the pole. Tansceusz did have the house painted while the wire was up, and we were concerned that the painter would notice the extra line, but he didn't. It would have been possible to use a radio transmitter instead of a hard wire, but transmitters had distance limitations and emanated a signal that could be detected and interfered with other devices. (This was state-of-the-art technology over thirty years ago.)

After the installation, the wiretap/bug had to be monitored and recorded by an agent, and it had to be done according to strict rules. All of those involved in the monitoring had to be briefed on the case and told who could be listened to. There is a statutory requirement of "minimization"—that is, only the persons who had been identified as subjects of the ELSUR could be monitored. If someone is heard who has not been identified as part of the conspiracy and who is not conversing with a known member of the conspiracy, they can't be monitored. The monitoring/recording machines were wired in such a way that if an agent could hear the conversation, it was recorded.

For each telephone line or bug, there were two recorders: one was the "original," and the tape was maintained as evidence; the other was a working copy. The working copy was used for review, and some "violation" conversations were transcribed. Logs were kept by the monitoring agents, and they showed on/off times, incoming/outgoing calls, summaries of conversations and "foot marks." The logs made it possible for anyone reviewing the tape to easily locate specific calls. A "five-day" report was usually required to be provided to the authorizing judge. The judge was then generally made aware of the status of the ELSUR and what evidence, if any, was being developed. In Tansceusz's case, the violation conversations, those that were related to drug trafficking, were used to help justify a thirty-day extension of the wire.

Tansceusz's wire ran for a total of sixty days. Tansceusz, as is often the case with a wire, became the best witness for the prosecution. He was careful when talking on the phone and was cryptic when discussing drugs, but he was candid in the "privacy" of his home. On several occasions, he said that he received and distributed forty pounds of pure cocaine per year. More specifically, Tansceusz told Rick Schrope, a friend and subdealer, that he would be getting six to seven pounds of "extra-high-quality coke" and would be charging more than his customary price of "nineteen" (price per ounce in the hundreds of dollars, or $1,900). Shrope said he would take a pound.

Less than a week after intercepting this conversation, on June 2, 1982, the FBI, DEA, IRS and police raided Tansceusz's home, pursuant to a search warrant. The affidavit for the search warrant cited conversations from the wire, but the search warrant was sealed. Tanceusz was still unaware of the wire when 1.6 pounds of pure cocaine was found in a "secret" compartment behind his medicine cabinet.

When the search was completed, Tanceusz was left with a copy of the search warrant and an inventory of what had been taken. But because the search warrant was sealed, he didn't get a copy of the affidavit, which contained the underlying probable cause for the search. The ELSUR coverage continued. The search, in effect, acted to "tickle the wire"; it caused Tansceusz to make incriminating telephone calls and statements overheard on the bug. Those conversations helped identify and strengthen the cases against Tansceusz's coconspirators.

After the search and the termination of the wire, all of the information gleaned from the wire was analyzed, and members of the conspiracy and other potential witnesses were interviewed. (Anyone recorded during the ELSUR who could be identified had to be given notice that they were intercepted.) The IRS began a "net worth" investigation of Tansceusz. He had no legitimate source of income, and from the wire, we learned that Tansceusz would buy uncut jewels, like rubies and emeralds, from Southeast Asia. Then it appeared that he tried to sell them for a profit to launder his drug profits.

Ultimately, Tansceusz was indicted, along with members of his conspiracy. His subdealers included the owner of a local Chrysler dealership and the owner of a popular restaurant near the University of Michigan campus. He was charged with operating a "continuing criminal enterprise," the severest federal drug trafficking statute. Conviction would have meant a mandatory minimum ten-year prison term but could have resulted in a life sentence.

On several occasions, while his conversations were being intercepted, Tansceusz had railed about drug dealers who had cut deals and testified against other dealers. He said he would never do that. Rather than go to trial, Tansceusz pleaded to lesser charges. He anticipated that he would be sentenced to less than five years. The judge sentenced him to ten years for cocaine distribution. (There is no parole in the federal system, so ten years means ten years.)

Drug dealer who refused to talk draws stiff prison sentence

JAMES TANCEUSZ
... got stiff sentence

By STEPHEN CAIN
NEWS STAFF REPORTER

Cocaine dealer James Gregory Tanceusz, claiming he was never as big in the business as his co-conspirators portrayed him, nonetheless drew a 10-year prison term and a $25,000 fine Wednesday from U.S. District Judge Charles W. Joiner in Ann Arbor.

The former Ann Arbor and Ypsilanti Township resident could have received up to 25 years and $535,000 in fines under the terms of the guilty pleas his lawyer negotiated with Justice Department Organized Crime Strike Force attorney Martin E. Crandall.

Still, it was the stiffest of 13 recent drug sentences handed out by Joiner, who has been criticized by a fellow federal jurist of imposing "absolutely ridiculous" low prison terms against major dealers.

One of the major reasons for the 10 years — rather than a lesser term — is that Tanceusz consistently refused to testify against his fellow dealers.

The 34-year-old Tanceusz, who trimmed his hair and beard and traded in casual dress for what he called the "stock broker look" of a

See SENTENCE, A4

Newspaper coverage of Tanceusz (photograph) sentencing, 1984. *Courtesy of the* Ann Arbor (MI) News.

The last time I saw Tansceusz, he was in a minimum-security federal correctional facility in Fort Worth, Texas. It wasn't hard time, but Tansceusz wasn't adapting well to prison. He had called and asked me to visit him, as he had information for me. When I visited him, he provided me with information about other drug dealers and said he would be willing to testify. Unfortunately, it was information we already had, so his testimony was of no value. Timing is everything—information is like groceries, it has a shelf life, and his was past the expiration date.

After the search of Tansceusz's home, he complained in an interview with the media that federal investigators had blatantly violated his Fourth Amendment rights. But this was no redux of the Webster Bivens case. Tansceusz learned that the game had changed, but we had followed the rules.

10
A TALE OF A GM EXECUTIVE WHO GOT BUSTED SELLING TEST CARS

Jack Clingingsmith had what any car guy would consider a dream job; he was the executive in charge of testing for Buick at the General Motors Proving Grounds. GM's Milford, Michigan Proving Ground, when it opened in 1924, was the auto industry's first dedicated testing facility. Today, the sprawling 400-acre complex has over one hundred buildings and about 132 miles (212 kilometers) of roads. Those roads replicate all types of conditions found on streets and highways throughout North America—from dirt tracks to four-lane interstate highways. There are also specialty surfaces to test traction, antiskid and brake technology.

In 1984, despite Clingingsmith having his dream job, he had serious personal financial problems. Part of Clingingsmith's duties was to dispose of test cars after they were no longer useful. Some of these cars were one-of-a-kind prototypes and some had experimental parts using developing technology. For obvious reasons, these cars were not to be sold or driven by unauthorized people. Consequently, the cars were to be destroyed by being crushed after they were no longer needed for testing. A crushed car, at that time, was worth about $90 as scrap metal. However, if the cars were sold for parts, they could bring $1,000 to $2,000 each.

Clingingsmith had a plan to alleviate his financial problems. He would sell the cars for parts rather than have them crushed; GM wouldn't know, and he could keep the difference. To do this, he would need to obtain phony documentation to show that the cars had been crushed. Part of the disposal process involved having the cars' vehicle identification number (VIN) plates

General Motors Proving Ground, Milford, Michigan. *Courtesy of General Motors.*

removed. Clingingsmith would turn in the VIN plates and advise GM and the Michigan secretary of state that the cars had been destroyed. In order to not deal with the scrap/auto parts dealers directly, Clingingsmith recruited an associate, Ingo Nicolay, to act as a middleman.

Nicolay was the general manager of Johnson Motors, a Pontiac dealership in Holly, Michigan. Clingingsmith knew Nicolay because Johnson Motors had, for years, done body work on cars that GM maintained for their executives. Nicolay agreed to participate in the scam and, in turn, recruited Donald Holloway, the owner of Holloway Auto Parts in Flint, a city just north of Holly and once the home of Buick. Holloway was more than willing to buy low-mileage, well-maintained used cars to be used for auto parts. He was also willing to provide fake bills of sale showing that the cars had been crushed.

Between November 1984 and December 1985, fourteen test cars (thirteen Buicks and one Oldsmobile) were reported to have been destroyed by Clingingsmith, but in actuality, they had been sold to Holloway for parts. The conspiracy seemed to be going well, and all of the conspirators were happy, but one of them was especially happy.

Holloway, on taking a delivery of these pristine used cars, had an epiphany: why disassemble these cars to sell for parts when they could be sold whole? The cars hadn't been reported stolen; in fact, there was no record that they even existed. But he thought that it probably wasn't wise to sell them locally.

Holloway had done business with a dealership, Fann's Auto Sales, in Manchester, Tennessee. He told the people at Fann's that he had a source for "assembled" GM cars. Assembled cars were cars that had been built from parts of two or more cars. (This was usually done with cars that had been extensively damaged in an accident.) For that reason, the VIN plates had been removed. There was a provision under Tennessee law that allowed for assembled cars to be registered and assigned new VINs. Fann's purchased the cars from Holloway for about $7,500 each. After registering the cars and receiving new VINs, Fann's sold them as assembled cars to unwary buyers. All would have been well, except one of the car buyers was working on his car and couldn't understand why one of the parts was not the part specified in the car's maintenance manual. He called GM to ask them about the part. The buyer was then connected with an engineer who realized that the questioned part had never been used in production. It was a test part.

All motor vehicles have public VIN plates. The most readily visible one is affixed to the dashboard, under the lower left side of the windshield. But vehicles also have discreet, or hidden, VINs; their locations are not generally known, and they are hard to remove. Using one of these VINs, it was found that the car in question was a test car and was supposed to have been destroyed. GM contacted the Michigan State Police (MSP), who learned, with the assistance of Tennessee police, that Fann's had purchased the car in question from Holloway in Flint, along with thirteen other cars. Because the cars had moved in "interstate commerce," between Michigan and Tennessee, MSP contacted the FBI.

The FBI interviewed Holloway, who was not initially forthcoming, but we convinced him it was in his best interest to cooperate. He disclosed that he had bought the cars from Nicolay. Holloway also said that he had provided Nicolay with documentation indicating that the cars had been crushed. The FBI then talked to Nicolay, who said that Clingingsmith had delivered the cars to him and that he had driven them to Holloway. Both Nicolay and Holloway admitted that they knew the cars had come from the GM Proving Grounds and were supposed to be destroyed. Finally, Clingingsmith was interviewed. He admitted that he had established the conspiracy and described his role in it. He thought Holloway had disassembled the cars and was surprised to learn they had been sold whole in Tennessee.

Because of the nature of the cars, they all had to be tracked down and seized. GM was willing to compensate the innocent buyers for the cars, but some of the buyers were reluctant to give them up. Two of the buyers were Tennessee state's attorneys, some were prosecutors and one was a Drug Enforcement Administration agent. Another buyer had bought a 1985 Buick Riviera convertible, a collector's item, as no Riviera convertibles were made in 1985. This one had been a hardtop that GM engineers had custom converted into a convertible. For a while, it was reportedly driven by Roger Smith, the CEO of GM (later vilified by Michael Moore in his documentary *Roger and Me*).

When the case was presented for prosecution, we realized there was a problem. What Clingingsmith had done with the cars was, legally speaking, not theft. We had initially planned to charge all three with conspiracy to transport stolen cars interstate under the Dyer Act. Instead, we found an alternative violation of a 1984 federal statute, "trafficking in motor vehicles without vehicle identification numbers" (18 USC § 2321).

In January 1987, Clingingsmith, Nicolay and Holloway pleaded guilty to conspiracy to traffic in motor vehicles without VINs. Because this was viewed as a less serious crime and the conspirators were first-time felons, they received relatively light sentences—less than a year of jail time with three years' probation, and they were required to pay about $60,000 in restitution.

Clingingsmith no longer had his dream job, and his financial woes had returned. Supposedly, the 1985 Buick Riviera custom convertible was destroyed.

11

UNMASKING THE JOKER

In the spring of 1989, a drama fraught with irony began playing out in Austria. A Jewish American family, a mother and her two grown sons, were fighting extradition to the United States. About fifty years before, Jewish families were desperately trying to leave Austria for safe havens like the United States. The subjects of the extradition were Linda Leary and her sons, Paul and Richard Heilbrunn. They fled to Austria from Indiana in anticipation of an indictment that was returned by a federal grand jury in November 1987.

The indictment was 136 pages long and contained fifty-three counts, variously charging thirty-four people. Paul and Richard were specifically charged with running a massive marijuana smuggling and distribution operation, legally termed a "continuing criminal enterprise" (CCE). According to the indictment, the ring operated from 1975 to 1985, distributed more than 150,000 pounds of marijuana and took in more than $50 million in cash. The figures were subsequently revised upward to 250,000 pounds of marijuana and $100 million. It would prove to be the largest marijuana ring ever prosecuted by the United States.

Paul Heilbrunn was characterized as the ringleader of the enterprise. Testimony later depicted him as both respected and feared. He was referred to as "Melech," Hebrew for king. Although Paul was a high school dropout, he was, by all accounts, a brilliant businessman. Prior to the indictment, he was believed to be a successful commodities trader in Indianapolis and wrote a column on trading for the local newspaper. He was a bon vivant who favored three-piece suits, frequented the finest restaurants and drove a top-of-the-line BMW. On several occasions, he rented jets and flew his friends to events, such as the Super Bowl and the NCAA Basketball Finals. Paul's older brother, Richard, on the other hand, was described as a big teddy bear. He lived on a farm and usually wore flannel shirts and jeans. Richard supervised operations, while Paul was the CEO.

Their mother, Linda Leary, was twice married and divorced, but she kept the name of her second husband. Leary was prominent in the Indianapolis community. She was the head of the Indiana League of Women Voters and president of the local chapter of the National Council of Jewish Women. Leary was also involved in her sons' business ventures. An early venture was dubbed Heilbrunn and Friends; ostensibly, it was a health food distribution business—a good front for marijuana distribution. The "friends" were high school buddies who had set up marijuana sales networks at the colleges they attended. But soon, the network was supplying customers outside of the campuses in eleven midwestern states. Most of the marijuana came by ship from Colombia, Jamaica and Thailand—an exotic global operation. It was then trucked to Indiana, where it was stored in barns that were owned or rented by the Heilbrunn organization.

Paul Heilbrunn had structured the organization so that information stove-piped—that is, information moved up and down, but only flowed between members as was necessary. This limited what any member could divulge should they choose to cooperate with law enforcement. Paul also had attorneys set up offshore corporations in the Bahamas and Panama to launder the proceeds from the marijuana operation. Linda Leary was designated as the head of several of these corporations. Much of the laundered money was transferred back into the Untied States and used to fund loans, often for Indiana businesses.

Today, the paradigm has changed; now, with so many states legalizing marijuana, it is almost like looking back on Prohibition. The Heilbrunns and their cohorts were not protesting the illegality of marijuana; rather, like the bootleggers, they were taking advantage of a restricted market. They could set the price, had little competition and the profits were tax free.

The beginning of the end for the Heilbrunn empire occurred in 1983, when a cocaine dealer was arrested. The dealer had previously worked for the Heilbrunns but had been let go for drug use. He offered to tell what he knew about the Heilbrunn operation as part of his plea bargain. There is no honor among thieves and little to none among drug dealers.

After the arrest of the cocaine dealer, law enforcement meticulously put together a case against the Heilbrunn organization, which culminated in the 1987 federal indictment. Most of the thirty-four people charged were known to the federal grand jury that returned the indictment, with the notable exception of one indictee who was referred to as "John Doe, also known as the Joker," like Batman's nemesis. There were also two female subordinates to the Joker; they were named as Jane Does, also known as "Tipper and Topper." (This was probably a disappointment to comic book purists who were anticipating a female code name like "Catwoman.")

While the Heilbrunns were fighting extradition, most of the indictees were prosecuted and convicted. Some cooperated and agreed to testify against others, including the Heilbrunns. In one of the coconspirator's trials, there was testimony about the Joker. He was depicted as "Paul Heilbrunn's trusted and valued peer," whose Michigan-based operation did business with Heilbrunn and his associates. But no one in the Heilbrunn organization other than Paul himself seemed to know Joker's true identity. One person in the Joker's organization had been identified and prosecuted for having stored a forty-thousand-pound load that had been purchased by the Joker from Heilbrunn. That person was James Shedd, who owned a barn in Ypsilanti Township, just southeast of Ann Arbor, where the load was stored. (Shedd had also previously been the manager of the Sidetrack Bar, a locally famous and historic reastaurant/bar in Ypsilanti.) Shedd had refused a plea deal and would not identify the Joker. That stand may have been based more on compensation from the Joker than honor.

It became a personal challenge for me to identify the Joker. It was a matter of pride. The Joker was a huge marijuana dealer who had been operating in my territory with impunity. There was an individual who had become disenchanted with the Joker's enterprise and reportedly had a falling out with him. I decided to see what, if anything, I could learn from him that might identify the Joker.

Over the next several months, the potential informant and I periodically met for coffee. We talked about a lot of things: sports, politics and, although nothing specific was discussed, drugs. Slowly, I gained his trust. I explained to him that I would never disclose his identity and that any information he provided me would be reported in such a way as to not divulge his identity. At no time did he ask me about any payment for information, nor did I offer him any compensation. We both understood that if he were to provide information, it would be because it was the right thing to do.

We began to discuss some specific things regarding marijuana distribution in Michigan. In early 1989, I asked him if he could help me identify the Joker. His reply was, yes, he could help—he could tell me who the Joker was: James Frederick Hill.

I immediately began to investigate James Hill. I found that Hill owned a house in an affluent part of Ann Arbor. He also owned a business in Ann Arbor, an ice cream shop on Main Street, The Lovin' Spoonful (sort of makes you wonder what was in the ice cream), and an eighty-acre farm just west of Ann Arbor. Hill had a master's degree from the University of Chicago. He had no criminal record, aside from an arrest for a traffic violation in 1973. It was nothing serious, but there was an arrest photograph. I sent a copy of the photograph to Indianapolis, and after seeing it, several of cooperating witnesses identified James Hill as the person they knew as the Joker.

Arrest photograph (mugshot) of James Frederick Hill. *Author's collection.*

Indianapolis obtained an arrest warrant for Hill, also known as the Joker. Early the next morning, we set up an arrest team at Hill's farm. When he was observed leaving the farm, we arrested him and took him to the Ann Arbor FBI Office. I explained to Hill that he had been identified as the Joker in a federal indictment from Indiana, charging him with multiple drug trafficking violations; I told him that he would be taken to Detroit to be arraigned and that he would likely remain in custody until he was transported to Indianapolis. He didn't really question anything and seemed to have expected to be arrested. He indicated that he would be cooperative but said he didn't want to be interviewed until he got to Indianapolis.

When the media learned of Hill/the Joker's arrest at the arraignment, they wanted to know how he had been identified. Rather than say nothing and encourage speculation, I made a statement that one of the cooperating witnesses in Indiana had identified him, which was partially true.

Hill was removed to Indiana and did cooperate. Tipper and Topper were identified as sisters Jennifer and Patricia Hanlon of Ann Arbor. They later pleaded guilty and were each sentenced to six years. In late 1989, the Heilbrunns lost their two-year fight against extradition and were returned

Lovin' Spoonful proprietor faces drug charges

Pot purchases earn 'Joker' 20 years

By STEPHEN CAIN
NEWS STAFF REPORTER

The Federal Bureau of Investigation's 16-month some Ann Arbor ... nearly ...

..., was taken into cu... by FBI agents at his 80-acre farm at 8930 Trinkle Road in Lima Township and then arraigned before U.S. Magistrate Thomas A. Carlson in Detroit. He was ordered held pending a bond hearing scheduled for 1 p.m. today in front of the magistrate.

The 1988 Ann Arbor City Directory lists Hill as the proprietor of the Lovin' Spoonful at 330 S. Main St. Washtenaw County Register of Deeds records list the property in his wife's maiden name, Terry L. Wolf.

The FBI says that Hill is the man listed as John Doe No. 1 or the "Joker" in a 136-page indictment issued Nov. 20, 1987, by a federal grand jury in Indianapolis, Ind.

The 34 defendants in the Indianapolis-based conspiracy imported and distributed more than 150,000 pounds of marijuana between September 1975 and November 1985 and took in more than $50 million in cash, according to the grand jury.

The indictment says the man who went under the name of Batman's arch enemy bought his first 100 pounds of pot from the Indiana group in April 1976 and then purchased an entire boatload that was smuggled into Biloxi, Miss., the following year. The grand jury did not say how much was on the boat.

The Joker allegedly received several 1,200- to 2,000-pound shipments during the intervening nine years. But between March 1985

...Joker received pounds, 40,000 pounds and a pair of 2,000-pound shipments.

All the marijuana was trucked to various locations in Washtenaw County, the indictment says.

The 40,000-pound load was stored in a barn owned by James G. Shedd at 1410 S. Grove Road, Ypsilanti Township. Shedd, the former manager of the Sidetrack bar in Ypsilanti, refused plea bargaining and would not identify the Joker, federal officials said.

He was sentenced to seven years in prison Dec. 2, 1988, after pleading guilty to conspiracy to import and distribute marijuana.

The only other persons who knew the Joker's true identity with certainty — chief conspirator Paul B. Heilbrunn, his brother and their mother — fled to Austria prior to the indictment, officials said.

FBI Special Agent Greg Stejskal, assigned to the Ann Arbor office, said one of the Indianapolis conspirators told investigators he had heard the Joker addressed as "Jim" and thought his last name might be something like "Hall."

Stejskal said he painstakingly eliminated the some two dozen Jim Halls who have listed phones or appear in other Washtenaw County records before checking out similar names, including Hill.

When he got to James F. Hill of Trinkle Road, certain things didn't add up — such as the address on his driver's license being the home of his wife's sister, the agent said.

"We ran a computer check and discovered a traffic bench warrant from 1973," said Stejskal. "He was arrested. His picture was taken and sent to Indianapolis, and we got a hit. They said, 'That's the Joker.'"

The FBI still is trying to identify two one-time Ann Arbor-based female colleagues of the Joker who, the indictment says, went under the code names "Tipper" and "Topper."

The Joker was named in nine separate counts of the 1987 indictment. The most serious charge, operating a continuing criminal enterprise, carries a mandatory minimum prison term of 10 years.

The charge also subjects Hill to possible forfeiture of all his property.

Newspaper coverage of James Hill's, also known as the Joker, arrest and headline of his sentence. *Courtesy of the* Ann Arbor *(MI)* News.

to the United States. In October 1990, Hill pleaded guilty and agreed to testify against the Heilbrunns. In his plea agreement, Hill admitted to having received several 1,200- to 2,000-pound shipments of marijuana, starting in 1976. Then, between March and November 1985, Hill received marijuana shipments of 18,000 pounds, 20,000 pounds, 40,000 pounds and a pair of 2,000-pound loads from the Heilbrunn organization. Hill said he made his last payment to Heilbrunn in 1986. By then, he had paid the Heilbrunn organization about $20 million for more than 100,000 pounds of marijuana.

James Hill was sentenced to twenty years in prison. Because he had pleaded to having run a continuing criminal enterprise, all of his assets were subject to forfeiture. The U.S. district court judge said that Hill would have received a harsher punishment without his cooperation. In January 1991, Linda Leary also pleaded guilty and agreed to testify against her sons. She was subsequently sentenced to nine years. There was no trial of the Heilbrunns. Paul and Richard pleaded guilty in April 1991, and in July 1991, they were sentenced. Richard received thirteen years in prison. Paul, the King, who had also pleaded guilty to running a CCE, received twenty-eight years in prison. Thus ended the Heilbrunn empire.

To my knowledge, no one ever learned the identity of the source who identified the Joker.

12

A CUBAN INMATE UPRISING, THE SALVATION ARMY AND SANTA'S HELPER

This is a Christmas story, but it really began just before Thanksgiving in 1987 at the federal penitentiary in Atlanta. The Cuban inmates had rioted and had taken control of a sizeable portion of the penitentiary. The catalyst for the riots happened years before that, in 1980.

The Mariel boatlift, a massive exodus of Cuban refugees from Cuba to the United States, had among its refugees convicted criminals. Fidel Castro had apparently thought the boatlift was an opportune time to relieve the overcrowding in his prisons. After arriving in the United States, those Cubans who were determined to be criminals were detained and placed in U.S. penitentiaries with no clear plan as to what to do with them in the long term. This uncertain future led, predictably, to unrest and, ultimately, the prison riots. When the inmates rioted and took control of part of the Atlanta Penitentiary, they also took some of the staff hostage.

The FBI was tasked with negotiating with the inmates and providing SWAT teams, should it become necessary to retake control of the penitentiary by force and rescue the hostages. SWAT teams from many of the nation's large offices were called to respond to Atlanta—our Detroit team was one of them. So, on a cold, rainy November night, an air force C-141 that was flying a circuit landed at Detroit Metro Airport to pick up our team. Already on board were teams from Pittsburgh and Cleveland. We arrived in Atlanta early the next morning.

The Atlanta Federal Penitentiary (1987)—note the complete destruction of the industries section of the penitentiary. *Author's collection.*

The Atlanta Penitentiary is a foreboding place. It was built in phases, beginning in the late 1800s and going into the first few decades of the 1900s. It has sixty-foot-high walls with watchtowers on each corner. On our arrival, we climbed to the top of one of the watchtowers and looked down into the prison yard. It looked like a scene from a postapocalyptic *Mad Max* movie. Inmates were walking around the yard, all carrying homemade weapons: long knives, swords, et cetera, made from scrap metal and sharpened on some of the prison's machines. After seeing that scene, we all assumed we were going to be in Atlanta for a while. We knew we would prevail if it came to having to use force—after all, they had made the critical tactical mistake of bringing knives to a gun fight—but they had hostages and a large supply of nonperishable food under their control.

The next morning, I was walking to the penitentiary's administration building for the shift change briefing when I saw a tent serving free coffee and Krispy Kreme donuts. It was the Salvation Army tent. The Salvation Army was there every day of the insurrection, including Thanksgiving, serving coffee, donuts, smiles and kind words. I've been on a lot of SWAT operations, but I had never been offered coffee, donuts or kind words from the neighborhood we were operating in. Knowing the Salvation Army was there for us had me thinking that I owed this selfless organization a debt—a pay-it-forward kind of thing.

The penitentiary insurrection was resolved peacefully after about two weeks through negotiation between the inmate leaders and FBI negotiators. The inmates' situation had become untenable. The key factor was that no social order was developed among the inmates, just anarchy. They went through several months' worth of food in just days. So, we all went back to our respective homes.

I did not forget the Salvation Army's generosity. I decided that every holiday season, for a few hours, I would volunteer to ring the bell and tend the red kettle in my hometown of Ann Arbor, Michigan. Some years later, I was ringing the bell at a local supermarket with my wife. We had both donned our Santa hats and were wearing the Salvation Army–issue red vests. It was snowing lightly, the Christmas lights were shining and carols were playing on the store's PA system. We were at one door of the store, greeting shoppers and collecting donations in our kettle, when all of a sudden, there was a commotion at the other door.

A man ran out of the store, closely followed by two other men in white butcher smocks. The men in the smocks tackled the man in the parking lot. They were trying to hold him down, but he was struggling and screaming as they pulled several cuts of meat from under his coat. The erstwhile meat thief continued to yell, flail and kick.

I turned to my wife and said, "I should probably go help them." I kept flex cuffs (large heavy-duty zip ties) in my car, so I grabbed some, walked over and knelt next to the struggling man. He was facing away from me. In my "soothing," authoritative voice that I used for arrests and reading someone their rights, I told him we could let him up but he needed to let me put these cuffs on him. The man turned his head to look at me, and his eyes got very big. I'm about six foot, four inches tall and weighed about 235 pounds at the time. I had forgotten I was wearing a Santa hat and a big red vest. After staring at me for a few moments, he asked, "Who are you?" I smiled and replied, "I'm Santa's helper." He immediately stopped fighting and struggling. He submissively allowed me to place the cuffs on him. The butchers and I stood him up, and he placidly waited for the police to arrive.

I have often thought there might be some profound Dickens-type message to be derived from this incident. I don't know if the meat thief was stealing prime rib for his family, sort of a protein version of Jean Valjean, or maybe he was planning to host a barbecue at a homeless enclave. There is certainly some irony in collecting donations for the Salvation Army at one door of a grocery store and, at the same time, having an economically disadvantaged meat thief fleeing from the other door. Maybe the message is as simple as this: if you're poor and hungry at Christmastime, there are places other than your local grocery store that you can go to that care, like the Salvation Army.

13

3:10 TO MARQUETTE

A Manhunt in the Northwoods of Michigan

In the summer of 1988, Vincent Loonsfoot, a Native American, drove to the Hannahville Potawatomi Reservation near Escanaba, Michigan. There, he ambushed and shot to death four members of his estranged wife's family before kidnapping her. Loonsfoot then set off into the woods, beginning a highly publicized manhunt through the almost impenetrable forest of Michigan's Upper Peninsula.

Michigan is made up of two peninsulas, the Upper and the Lower. The Upper Peninsula (UP) extends east from Wisconsin and is bounded to the north by Lake Superior. The Lower Peninsula, the larger of the two, looks like a mitten, so Michiganders tend to point to their hand when giving directions. The Lower Peninsula is bound by Lake Michigan to the west and Lake Huron to the east. The shortest distance between the two peninsulas, the Straits of Mackinac, is where the two lakes meet at the top of the Lower Peninsula. For years, the only way to get from one peninsula to the other was by boat or plane. In 1957, the Mackinac Bridge was finished, allowing for car and truck traffic between the two.

Although the two peninsulas are now connected, they remain dramatically different. In some ways, the UP remains the pristine wilderness immortalized in Longfellow's epic poem *Hiawatha*: "By the shores of Gitche Gumee" was Longfellow's way of describing the Lake Superior Coast of the UP.

Vincent Loonsfoot and his wife, Peggy, were living near Baraga on the Keweenaw Bay Reservation. An Ojibwa tribal court awarded Peggy sole custody of the Loonsfoots' two-year-old daughter, based on a finding

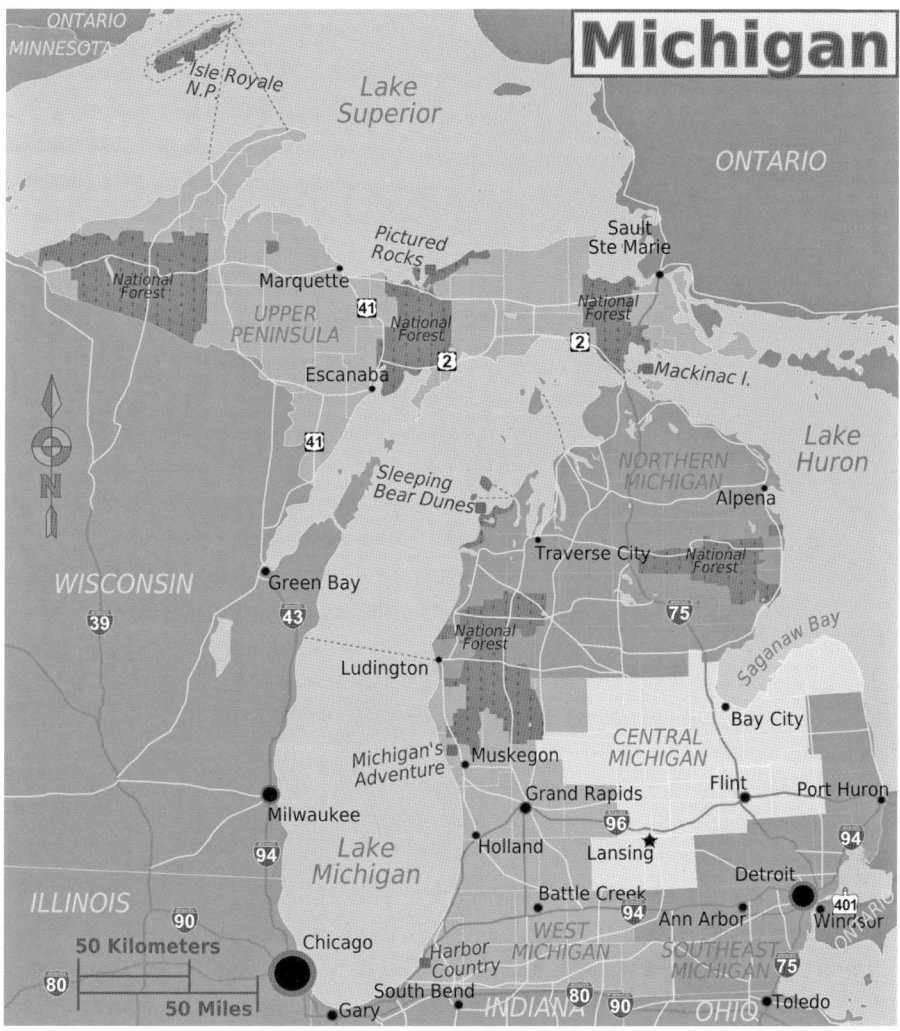

A map of the upper and lower peninsulas of Michigan. *Courtesy of Peter Fitzgerald, Wikimedia Commons.*

that Loonsfoot had repeatedly physically abused Peggy. Peggy was afraid of Loonsfoot, so without telling him, Peggy moved with their daughter to Escanaba on the south/Lake Michigan side of the UP. Loonsfoot followed her, but not being certain where she was staying, he staked out the home of her brother David Smith on the Hannahville Reservation, near Escanaba. While waiting for Smith and his family to return, Loonsfoot used cocaine and drank beer.

It is not clear if Loonsfoot had a plan, but when the Smith family came home, he ambushed them. Using David Smith's rifle, Loonsfoot shot and killed David, his wife and two of their daughters, ages two and eleven. He wounded a third daughter, Amanda, age ten. Loonsfoot, driving the Smiths' car, then forced Amanda to take him to the home where Peggy (her aunt) was staying. There, Loonsfoot kidnapped Peggy, leaving Amanda behind. (Amanda would recover from her wounds.) Loonsfoot drove to a ski area outside of Escanaba, where the car stalled. Then Loonsfoot set off into the woods with Peggy, who was barefoot and three months pregnant. He had no provisions and only the clothes they were wearing. However, he did have Smith's .30-caliber lever-action rifle and some knives.

Because the murders had occurred on a Native American reservation, the crimes fell under federal jurisdiction. The Marquette FBI office was notified. (Marquette is the largest city in the UP and is on Lake Superior.) When the Marquette FBI agents were able to assess the situation, they called the main Michigan FBI office in Detroit. It was decided that the FBI SWAT team would be dispatched to the UP to conduct a search for Loonsfoot and Peggy. In the meantime, state and county law enforcement were attempting to cordon off the area around Escanaba to keep Loonsfoot from escaping.

The FBI SWAT team was flown to the UP in an air force national guard C-130. I was a SWAT team leader but was in the midst of a trial in which I was case agent, so I couldn't deploy until it was concluded. The SWAT team was on the ground and searching within forty-eight hours of the murders/abduction. The trail was cold, and the woods were extremely thick. Tracking dogs were able to pick up a scent. It appeared Loonsfoot was using railroad right-of-ways but would periodically go into the woods to avoid detection. Trains leaving the area were searched. Aircraft were also used in the search, but they had not made any sightings. Loonsfoot seemed to have been moving in a westerly direction from Escanaba. Making the search more difficult, it was the height of the blackfly season, and the woods were full of voracious ticks. The SWAT guys made a game of picking ticks off each other at the end of the day, seeing who had collected the most.

There were several possible sightings of Loonsfoot and Peggy by local residents and reports of eggs being pilfered from local farms. The response to these sightings had not resulted in any confirmation of Loonsfoot's past or present locations.

The search had been ongoing for about a week when my trial ended. The following day, I headed for the UP. It was over four hundred miles from my home in Ann Arbor to Escanaba, not as the crow flies, but I had to drive my

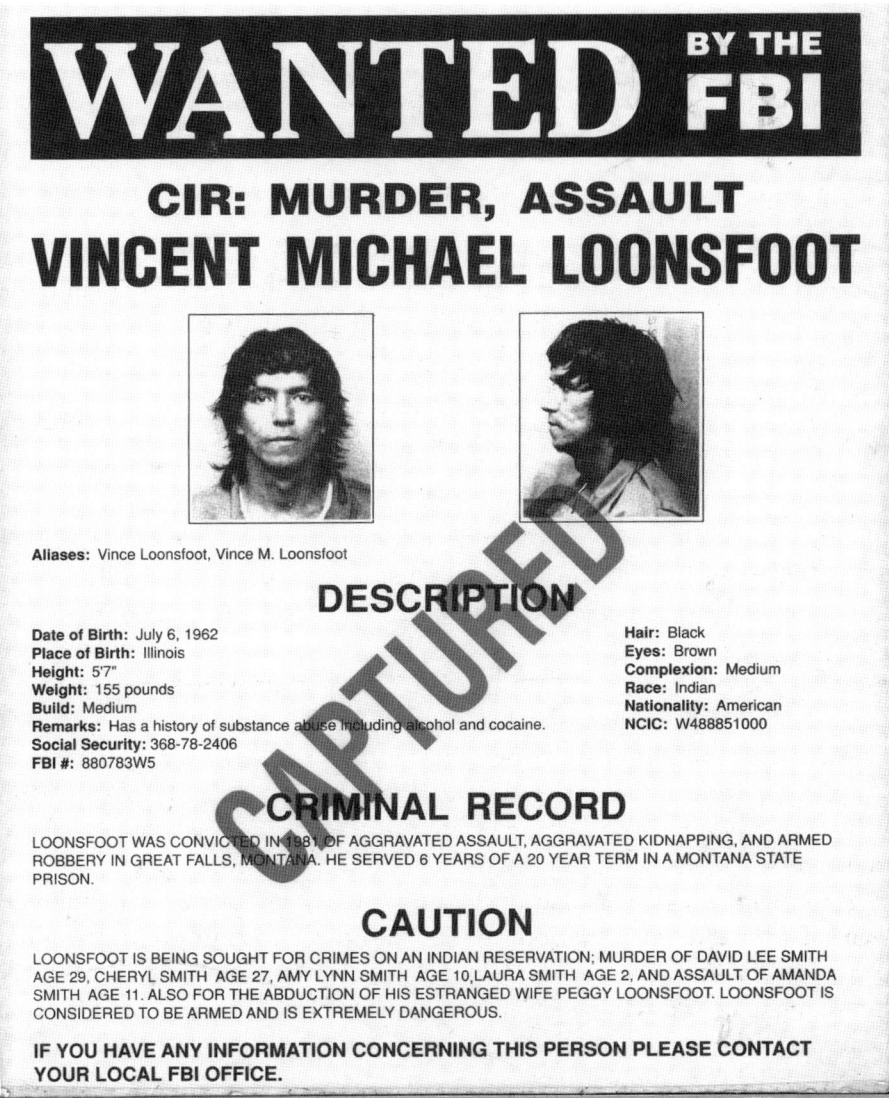

FBI wanted poster for Vincent Loonsfoot (1988). *Author's collection.*

bureau car and cross the Mackinac Bridge to get there. When I arrived in Escanaba, I saw some of the SWAT team guys near the county fairgrounds. I stopped, and they filled me in on the status of the search. They had just finished checking the area based on a sighting but hadn't found anything. They directed me to the command post.

At the command post, I met with Jerry Craig, the overall SWAT team leader. Jerry gave me a tour of the area, showing me where the murders occurred and where Loonsfoot had left the car and entered the woods over a week before. I also learned that the full search would be terminated the following day, leaving me in charge, along with three SWAT guys who volunteered to stay, Steve Hancock, Bill Randall and Chuck Smith. We would act as a roving patrol to respond to sightings or other indications that our quarry may be at a location. There was some doubt that Loonsfoot and/or Peggy were still in the area or were still alive. One non-SWAT agent at the command post suggested I be alert for congregations of crows or buzzards, as it might be evidence of human carrion—a logical tip until you consider how many dead animals there are in the north woods.

The next day, I had a sinking feeling as I watched the C-130 rise from Escanaba Airport. I was then in charge of a four-man team searching for an armed and extremely dangerous Native American man and his hostage somewhere in the vast woods of the UP. I went back to the command post. All of the media and their satellite antenna trucks were gone. I reviewed the maps, checking the locations of the sightings, et cetera. It did seem that most of the recent sightings, if they were accurate, were relatively close to town, but it was difficult to connect the dots.

I went to dinner with my team and explained to them what our mission would be starting the next morning. After dinner, we all went back to our hotel, knowing we would start early the next day. I had no idea how early. At around 3:00 a.m., I was awakened by a call from an FBI supervisor who had received a call from the sheriff's office in Escanaba. Loonsfoot, with Peggy, had just walked into the sheriff's office. Loonsfoot had indicated that he wanted to surrender. I called Bill Randall, and we drove to the sheriff's office. The other two SWAT agents would follow as quickly as they could. There was only one other person at the sheriff's office, the dispatcher; he was in a room separated from the reception area by protective glass. The dispatcher did not want to leave his enclosure for fear that Loonsfoot's intent was less than honorable.

Bill and I approached the sheriff's office carefully. We were able to see through a window Loonsfoot and Peggy sitting placidly on a bench in the reception area. We entered with guns drawn and ordered Loonsfoot to the floor. He offered no resistance. We handcuffed and searched him. Loonsfoot was shirtless, and we noted with some satisfaction that he was dirty and badly bug bitten. We also talked to and, as unobtrusively as possible, searched Peggy, just to make sure she hadn't succumbed to Stockholm syndrome (when a captive becomes sympathetic to their captor). Peggy looked very tired but seemed to be in relatively good shape and relieved that her ordeal was over. We had the dispatcher call for medical assistance for her.

Later that morning, the agents from Marquette arrived to interview Loonsfoot, as they would be handling the federal prosecution. I sat in on the interview, as Loonsfoot was my responsibility until we turned him over to the U.S. Marshal. In the interview, Loonsfoot matter-of-factly confessed to ambushing and killing the Smith family and kidnapping Peggy. It was as though he was discussing a baseball game from the day before. He showed no emotion and seemed to have no regret. He talked about his first day and night in the woods. He and Peggy had walked to a highway rest stop west of Escanaba. There, Loonsfoot waited all night for a car to arrive. If one had stopped, he intended to kill the driver and any occupants and take the car. He waited all night for a car, but none stopped. Only an eighteen-wheeler pulled into the rest stop, but Loonsfoot didn't know how to drive a big truck. That truck driver will never know how lucky he was.

Loonsfoot never made it farther than the rest stop. He and Peggy had doubled back and spent the rest of their time on the run near town. During that time, he retrieved scraps of food from garbage cans. One night, when it was raining, they slept in a dumpster. Loonsfoot was not a skilled woodsman, just an urban Native American.

During the interview, Loonsfoot looked at me and said:

> *I saw you a couple of days ago by the county fairgrounds. You were standing by a white car* [my bureau car] *and talking to some guys with rifles, wearing vests and helmets. You weren't wearing a vest or helmet. I had you in my sights, and I was going to shoot you and take your car. But I knew if I did the guys with the rifles would have got me.*

As with that unknown truck driver, the angel of death had apparently passed me over, too.

I asked him where his rifle was. He said it was in a field behind a grocery store not too far from the fair grounds. At first light, Bill Randall and I drove to field, and within minutes, we found the lever-action rifle. It still had a round in the chamber. That bullet had special significance for me.

When we got back to the sheriff's office with the rifle, the media had returned, as had the hierarchy from the FBI office in Detroit. There was also a crowd of local citizens, many of them Native Americans. It was my responsibility to arrange for Loonsfoot's transfer to Marquette, where there was a federal district court and a U.S. Marshal who would take custody of Loonsfoot and hold him for prosecution. Marquette is about sixty-five miles north of Escanaba. I was concerned for Loonsfoot's safety. I was feeling like Van Heflin's character in the movie *3:10 to Yuma*, having to transport a notorious bad guy, knowing his gang was waiting to spring him (in a later version of the movie, Christian Bale plays the part); only, those Native Americans in the crowd outside didn't want to help Loonsfoot to escape—they wanted revenge. He had killed most of a Native American family from their community.

My plan was to use three vehicles. The two agents from Marquette would be in the lead car, as they were familiar with the route. I would put Loonsfoot in the second car with the other three SWAT agents who would be armed with automatic weapons. I would be in the tail car with my Remington 870, literally riding shotgun. I planned to load the cars in a large garage that was attached to the sheriff's office and then just drive out, en route to Marquette. But I was overruled, as the media wanted a "perp walk" outside. We would just have to put a Kevlar vest on Loonsfoot, walk him to the car and hope there were no Jack Rubys (potential assassins) in the crowd. The whole transport operation went smoothly, although I kept thinking about contingencies, like a big tree lying in the road, portending an ambush.

After turning Loonsfoot over to the U.S. Marshal, we returned to Escanaba. The sense of relief in the town was palpable. There was no longer an armed killer lurking in the woods. We went out to dinner and stayed to celebrate. We didn't buy our own drinks all night. It seemed like every guy in town wanted to shake our hand, and every girl wanted to give us a hug. I felt guilty about accepting this adulation, having arrived late to the manhunt, but I felt it was my duty to take one for the team.

Trial and Tribute

In December 1988, Loonsfoot was tried before a U.S. District Court judge in Marquette. The judge found him guilty of four counts of first-degree murder, as well as kidnapping. In February 1989, Loonsfoot was sentenced to life in prison with no chance of parole. The judge could have imposed the death penalty under federal law, even though Michigan has never had a death penalty.

Peggy Deleon (formerly Loonsfoot) is now remarried and still lives in the Escanaba area. She gave birth to a healthy son, with whom she was pregnant at the time she was abducted.

I want to pay tribute to all the FBI agents who have volunteered to become members of the FBI SWAT program. They must undergo testing, qualify and participate in extensive periodic training. They are subject to being "called out" without notice and spend time away from home. These assignments, by nature, are dangerous and can cause hardships for the agents and their families—all for no extra pay. SWAT agents exemplify the FBI motto: "Fidelity, Bravery, Integrity."

14

MARK FROM MICHIGAN

*The Rise and Fall of a Founder
of the Michigan Militia Movement*

Mark and I never really hit it off.

I first met Mark Koernke in the late 1980s. Gene Ward, a fellow FBI agent, had asked me to accompany him on an interview of Koernke. We met with him in his basement office at Alice Lloyd Hall, a University of Michigan dormitory, where he was a janitor. At the time, Ward was investigating a potential hate crime, the painting of some racial epithets on a home. It had been suggested that Koernke might know something about it. (Koernke was a proponent of White supremacy ideology.) Koernke denied that he had any knowledge of it, and we concluded that he probably had no connection to the graffiti painting.

During the interview, Koernke made it known that he had been an intelligence officer in the army, and in addition to that, he said he was a counterintelligence expert. He said he continued to train U.S. military units in the tactics of foreign militaries. I made my skepticism of Koernke's background no secret and questioned some of his conspiracy theories that he apparently felt compelled to share with us. This all predated Koernke's seminotoriety that he later gained as "Mark from Michigan" and from his own radio show, *The Intelligence Report*.

He was an early purveyor of the "New World Order," which he believed was a worldwide conspiracy. As best as I have been able to understand, the New World Order involves the takeover of the United States by the United Nations, which is fronting for some insidious international cabal that wants to institute international socialism. (I think there was considerable borrowing from such works as *The Protocols of the Elders of Zion*.) Part of this conspiracy was the building of secret concentration camps in the western United States to house those who would be unwilling to accept the New World Order. Among other things, he believed "black helicopters" were being used to spy on Americans. The black helicopters and "Mark from Michigan" became synonymous. The New World Order was supposed to have taken over by now, but it hasn't, and maybe that's because Koernke has been on watch. I think Koernke perceived himself to be the "intellectual" underpinning of the militia movement, sort of a latter-day Thomas Paine.

Anyway, our paths continued to cross. There were the times I saw him surveilling the federal building parking lot. I guess he was trying to log our movements for intelligence purposes. I would wave to him, and he would hide.

During the late 1980s and early 1990s the militia movement grew dramatically. The high-water mark came soon after the bombing of the Murrah Federal Building in Oklahoma City. Many people in the movement were shocked and disgusted by the slaughter of innocent people, including children. They did not want to be identified with a philosophy that condoned such acts. (In contrast, Koernke espoused the theory that the government actually did the bombing to set up Timothy McVeigh and to destroy records that proved the "Gulf War Syndrome" was real. He didn't really explain why those records were in Oklahoma City.)

As the militia movement diminished, there were some internal conflicts. In 1997, in Michigan, one member of the militia was murdered, and other members were charged with the murder. Although Koernke was never believed to have been involved, he was subpoenaed to be a witness. When a process server showed up on Koernke's porch, an argument ensued. Apparently, Koernke threatened the server with a rifle, resulting in Koernke being charged with assault with a dangerous weapon. Koernke's trial date was set for May 1998, but when Koernke didn't appear for the trial, a bench warrant was issued for his arrest. In June, a federal fugitive warrant for Koernke was issued, based on my affidavit stating that there was reason to believe he had fled from Michigan.

While Koernke was a fugitive, he continued his shortwave radio broadcasts from various undisclosed locations. He mentioned me several times in unflattering terms. He also said that unless the federal charges were dropped, "a lot of their [FBI] people might get hurt."

The following July, a Michigan State Police helicopter was searching for marijuana growing plots in rural Barry County, just north of Battle Creek, Michigan, when its crew observed a pickup truck and a man and a woman near an abandoned mobile home. When the helicopter came in for a closer look, the man, Koernke, began running. I don't know if the helicopter was black, but it must have been unsettling for Koernke to have a helicopter seemingly coming for him. Koernke then jumped into a shallow lake, where only his head was showing. (Presumably, Koernke was looking for a hollow reed so he could breathe while submerged like in so many old movies.)

When the police ground units arrived, Koernke was persuaded to come out of the water—but not before giving a one-finger salute. Koernke told the police he was Michael Kerns. He was affecting an Irish brogue and had attempted to dye his hair red, although the result was closer to orange. Several weapons were found in the pickup truck, including an AR-15 and a semi-automatic AK-47. Kerns/Koernke was taken into custody and lodged in the Barry County Jail in Hastings.

It was suspected that Kerns might be Koernke, but a positive identification would take hours, as there was not yet a way to electronically transmit fingerprints to locations where his prints were on file. That night, the Barry County Sheriff called me and asked if I could come to his jail to identify Koernke, as I was the affiant on the federal fugitive warrant. When I arrived at the Barry County Sheriff's Office, there sat Mark Koernke with orange hair and no mustache. I greeted Mark by name, but he acted as if he didn't know me and spoke in a terrible Irish brogue. He said his name was Michael Kerns. I told him that I needed to ask him a few questions, but first, I had to advise him of his rights. After advising him, I passed him the acknowledgement form and asked him to sign it, which he did. I looked at the form and asked him if he realized he had signed the form "Mark Koernke." He looked totally crestfallen.

In August 1999, after being placed on bond again, Koernke was tried on the assault charge and found guilty. The judge sentenced him to eighty days in jail, but he was credited with time served and given probation.

Koernke continued his shortwave broadcasts and began hawking his videocassettes with titles like *America in Peril* to a somewhat diminished audience. But our paths were destined to cross one more time.

In March 2000, there was a bank robbery in downtown Dexter, Michigan, Koernke's hometown. I responded to the robbery and was en route when I heard radio traffic describing a suspect vehicle, a 1985 white Plymouth Fury. A sheriff's deputy had stopped a car matching that description, but when he approached the car, it sped off. A high-speed chase ensued that lasted for forty minutes. During the chase, the officers became aware that the car was Mark Koernke's, and he appeared to be driving it. The police were able to

Militiaman gets prison for evasion

By LIZ COBBS
NEWS STAFF REPORTER

Militia activist Mark Koernke was sentenced to at least three years in prison for running away from police during a chase last year.

Koernke, 43, of Webster Township, appeared Monday before Washtenaw County Circuit Judge Melinda Morris amid tight security in the courtroom and around the courthouse building.

Koernke's attorney, Daniel Hunter of Ypsilanti, asked Morris to follow a sentencing recommendation of six months in jail and three years on probation.

Morris said she would not follow the recommendation because of Koernke's felony conviction two years ago stemming from a similar offense.

Hunter said he had recommended that Koernke's sentence be a year or less so that he would serve time in jail, rather than prison. This is Koernke's second felony conviction and his first time receiving a prison sentence.

"I think everybody was caught up in the emotion of things rather than in what went on," Hunter said this morning. "My experience is everybody wants this to be bigger than what it really is."

When the judge asked Koernke whether he wanted to make a statement before she sentenced him, he replied, "No."

Hunter said he could not talk to Koernke immediately after the hearing because Washtenaw County Sheriff's deputies took Koernke from the courtroom and back to jail.

Morris sentenced Koernke to 2-6 years in

See **KOERNKE, Back Page**

KOERNKE

Militia activist Mark Koernke's previous criminal conviction prompted a judge to send him to prison for up to 7.5 years.

Here's his sentence:
- Three to 7.5 years for fleeing a police officer.
- 21 months to three years for resisting and obstructing an officer.
- Two to six years on two charges of assault with a dangerous weapon.

Newspaper coverage of Koernke's (photograph) sentencing (2001). *Courtesy of the Ann Arbor (MI) News.*

cut off Koernke. He tried to ram a police car and run over a deputy. Then he decided to drive cross-country across a field, but he ended up hitting a tree. He got out and ran toward a channel of a lake. There, he again executed his water escape and evasion tactic, swimming across the channel. The police caught up to him on the other side.

As an MSP trooper with his gun drawn approached Koernke, Koernke shoved him. The trooper displayed remarkable restraint and didn't shoot him but rather subdued and handcuffed Koernke. I proceeded to the bank and quickly learned Koernke was not the bank robber. (We later caught the actual bank robber, who was responsible for several other robberies.)

Apparently, Koernke, a customer of the bank, had stopped in the street in front of the bank and had his son get out of the car to place a deposit in the bank's ATM. The son, after making the deposit, ran back to the car. He was wearing a baseball cap, as was the bank robber. Witnesses outside the bank saw this, and when they were questioned about the bank robbery, thinking they had witnessed the getaway they gave a description of Koernke's car. After the description was broadcast, Koernke was stopped and then chased when he fled.

It is not clear to me why Koernke fled from the police. There were no helicopters up that day. He later claimed that he feared for the safety of his two sons who were in the car, but they remained in the car for a good portion of the high-speed chase. (Koernke had them get out of the car before he was forced to stop.)

In March 2001, Koernke was convicted of fleeing from the police, assault with a dangerous weapon (his car) and resisting and obstructing. The trial and sentencing were set before the same judge as his first trial. But the judge was far less sympathetic this time. She sentenced him on each count to run concurrently, with seven years being the maximum time in prison. He would have served about three years if he had been paroled, but he did not get along well in prison and did close to the maximum time.

On March 15, 2007, Koernke completed his sentence. He resumed his shortwave broadcasts of *The Intelligence Report*, most recently carried on Liberty Tree Radio. In addition, he has many videos available on YouTube. I haven't heard anything from Koernke recently, including during the Michigan Militia's much-publicized alleged conspiracy to kidnap the governor of Michigan in 2020.

15
A TALE OF UNION RACKETEERING OR HOW I LEARNED TO LOVE THE HOBBS ACT

Richard Debs was the president of United Auto Workers (UAW) Union Local 1776 (no relation to Eugene V. Debs, the union organizer and socialist from the early twentieth century). Debs had been the president of the local for fifteen years in 1988. Local 1776 represented the workers at the General Motors Willow Run Assembly Plant near Ypsilanti, Michigan, where Chevrolet Impalas were made. Debs liked that job, and authorities suspected he was willing to harm people to keep it. But before I get into that, some history of the Willow Run Plant.

Willow Run was a massive industrial complex first developed by Ford during World War II to make the B24 Liberator bombers. At that time, it was the largest assembly line facility in the world. At its peak, it turned out a bomber every fifty-five minutes and was home to Rosie the Riveter (the model for the iconic picture worked at the plant). After the war, GM acquired the complex, expanded and converted it into an assembly plant and built another plant for the construction of the GM Hydra-matic transmissions.

During the waning halcyon days of the American auto industry, as the president of a local, Debs had considerable power over a fiefdom that comprised all the workers at the assembly plant. Debs did not work at the plant; rather, he administered the local from an office in a union building near the plant. Because all of GM's plant jobs required UAW membership, Debs had the ability to influence hiring and disperse jobs. He also had political power in the local community that derived from his position. There were also ample opportunities for corruption and graft to those so inclined.

Periodically, UAW local officers must stand for reelection, and there was to be an election in the spring of 1989. Debs was being challenged for the presidency by two other local members, Jesse Gray and Bob Harlow. Despite Debs's fifteen years as the president, he was not universally liked. He had also recently been charged, albeit acquitted, in a federal corruption case involving a local judge. (The judge and several others were convicted.)

In the fall of 1988, the FBI learned from a "walk-in" source that Debs had been attempting to hire some men to dissuade, by violence, Gray and Harlow from running against him. The source knew the identities of some of the men who had been approached by Debs, but he/she did not know whether anyone had agreed to Debs's plan. Although the source's information was deemed creditable, it was not clear whether Debs had progressed beyond the solicitation stage, and we did not want to jeopardize the source.

It was decided that the best course of action was to advise the Michigan State Police (MSP) and the potential victims of the information. We arranged to have Jesse Gray and Bob Harlow come to the MSP post in Ypsilanti, which was the post responsible for the Willow Run complex. There, Gray and Harlow were apprised of the alleged threat. They were also advised to take some precautions, like avoiding predictable routines and varying their routes to and from work.

About a month after the meeting with Gray and Harlow, Gray was shot in the neck while driving to work in the early morning of December 29. Gray was not killed, but multiple shots had been fired at his truck from a pickup as it passed him. Gray was unable to give more than a general description of the pickup. He thought there was more than one person in the pickup, but he could not provide any descriptions. MSP conducted the crime scene investigation and was able to recover several spent 9-mm slugs from Gray's vehicle, including the one that struck Gray. Although Gray's wound was not life-threatening, it was serious, and it had to be concluded that the shooter intended to kill Gray.

As a result of the shooting, Gray dropped out of the race for presidency of the UAW local. Bob Harlow decided to continue his effort to unseat Debs, but he confided that, following our warning, he had varied his route to and from work. Gray had not.

MSP and the FBI began an investigation of the shooting. We interviewed Debs, but he denied any involvement in the shooting and said he and his wife were in Cleveland visiting family at the time. Debs also denied soliciting anyone to harm either Gray or Harlow. During the investigation, we heard rumors of Debs having unusually close relationships with young men and boys. (That would foreshadow some future events.) We interviewed one of the young men—I will refer to him as John—who said that Debs had befriended him and given him money and gifts, but he denied being asked by Debs to harm anyone. When asked about his whereabouts at the time of the shooting, John said he was in Cleveland with Debs. John elaborated and said that late on the night of December 28, Debs and his wife came to John's apartment. Debs said he would pay John to drive them in Debs's car to Cleveland. They drove to Cleveland and arrived early in the morning on the December 29. Debs had John drop them off at a house and told him to pick them up at 11:00 a.m. When John picked them up, Debs had him drive them back to Michigan. Debs never explained to John why he and his wife needed to go to Cleveland late at night and, a few hours later, return home.

As an investigator, you question coincidences. Why would Debs, seemingly on the spur of the moment, decide to travel to Cleveland hours before the shooting of Jesse Gray and then return only hours later? I remembered an adage from the book of Proverbs: "The wicked flee when none pursueth," (Proverbs 28:1).

In April, Debs was defeated by Bob Harlow for the presidency of local 1776.

It had been months since the shooting, and we were not any closer to identifying the shooters or tying Debs to the shooting. MSP had to cut back on its involvement. We had done most of the investigation, and without new leads, a resolution didn't seem too promising. We had interviewed some of the individuals the source said had been approached by Debs to dissuade Gray and Harlow from running against him, but all of them had been eliminated as the actual shooters. We were able to confirm that four of the five men had been approached by Debs and offered jobs and/or money to violently dissuade Gray and Harlow from running against him. The four we interviewed had refused Debs's offer. There hadn't been any further discussion as to what specific violence Debs had in mind. I came away from those interviews unenthusiastic about how creditable those four men would be to a jury. When you try to recruit some men to commit felonies of violence, you don't go looking for Eagle Scouts.

I didn't think I would bring the case any closer to a resolution, but I decided to interview the fifth man Debs had reportedly contacted. The fifth man, Larry Poore, said Debs had made the same proposal to him that he had made to the others. Poore said his initial response to Debs was he didn't even know Bob Harlow. So, Debs gave Poore a photograph of him. Poore told Debs he would think about it, but he said he never had any intention of doing anything. Later, he told Debs he didn't want to do it.

As I was getting ready to leave Poore's home, he asked me if I wanted the photograph Debs had given him of Harlow—I hadn't thought to ask, but the photograph had potential to be a great windfall. I very carefully placed the photograph into an evidence envelope. The next day, I sent it to the FBI Labratory with a request that it be examined for fingerprints. Any latent fingerprints that were found would be compared with the fingerprints of Poore and Debs. I was not optimistic, but it was worth a shot. When I received the lab report, it stated there were only two legible fingerprints on the photograph: one was Larry Poore's, and the other was Richard Debs. I felt like I had just drawn to an inside straight. We had physical evidence to corroborate Poole's account of Debs's solicitation, which indirectly corroborated the other four men's similar statements.

I knew we still could not prove that Debs had any connection to the shooting of Jesse Gray, but we could show that Debs, prior to the shooting, had attempted or conspired to commit violence against Harlow and Gray. Because this conspiracy's goal was to impede UAW members from running for office, it denied the member electorate a choice. Also, because a conspiracy was alleged, the rules regarding hearsay evidence didn't apply to statements in furtherance of the conspiracy.

In late fall 1989, a federal grand jury returned a four-count indictment, charging Debs under the Hobbs Act (18 USC § 1951) with having "solicited five different men to do wrongful violence against Bob Harlow and Jesse Gray" in an attempt to frighten them away from running against Debs for the UAW local presidency. (The Hobbs Act was enacted as a statute to combat racketeering in labor-management disputes and corruption directed at members of labor unions.) A fourth count of the indictment actually charged that "Debs caused Jesse Gray to be shot for the purpose of inducing him and other union members not to oppose Debs in the 1989 election." We knew we would have difficulty proving Debs's involvement in the shooting, but by charging it, we could make the jury aware of the shooting and Debs's coincidental "flight" to Cleveland.

Pursuant to the indictment, we arrested Debs at his home. He was in bed, and on his nightstand was a loaded .38-caliber revolver. When we arraigned Debs, the government asked for detention, but he was released on a $25,000 bond, despite the nature of the charges. In September 1990, Debs pleaded guilty to one count of the indictment. Debs was allowed to stay on bond until his sentencing.

In November, while awaiting sentencing, Debs was arrested and charged with first-degree criminal sexual conduct after allegedly forcing a twelve-year-

Indictment: Debs tried to hire attackers
Rivals were alleged targets

By JUDSON BRANAM and PHIL CACKLEY
NEWS STAFF REPORTERS

Former Ypsilanti UAW leader Richard Debs faces a court hearing next week after he was indicted Monday for trying to hire five different men to attack two union rivals in late 1988.

Debs, who was arrested by FBI agents on the four-count federal grand jury indictment Monday, also offered to use his influence as president of United Auto Workers Local 1776 to get jobs back for the laid-off workers he tried to hire, union sources told The News.

The 52-year-old Westland resident, who lost his job as union president at the General Motors assembly plant in an April election, denied the charges and said he wasn't connected to the Dec. 29, 1988, shooting of Jesse Gray, who was plant bargaining chairman.

"The allegations are false," he told The News after he was arraigned in U.S. District Court in Detroit. "You'll find out once we get into court that it's all horse—."

He claimed the charges were a vendetta by an FBI agent and union officials out to get him.

RICHARD DEBS
... pleads not guilty

The grand jury indictment unsealed Monday alleges Debs solicited five different men to "do wrongful violence" against Bob Harlow, Local 1776 vice president, and Gray in an attempt to frighten them away from running against Debs for the UAW local presidency.

None of those men was indicted by the grand jury and none of the five ever carried out any plans, according to the indictment.

No charges are pending against anyone else in the case, said Assistant U.S. Attorney Keith E. Corbett, who is handling the trial. The men, whose names are given in the indictment, are expected to be prosecution witnesses.

According to the indictment, Debs sought out, in late November or early December 1988, Larry Poore, 33, of Ypsilanti Township in his bid to frighten Harlow and Gray.

Two other pairs of Ypsilanti area men, Jeffrey and Michael Hammond, and Donald and Charles Varney, also allegedly were recruited in November 1988 to attack Harlow, who unseated Debs from the post he had 15 years in the vote last April by the 4,350-member local.

Union sources, who asked not to be named, said Debs allegedly

See DEBS, A13

FBI/DOJ

Newspaper coverage of Debs's (photograph) indictment (1989). *Courtesy of the* Ann Arbor *(MI)* News.

old boy to perform oral sex on him. Afterward, he had to await sentencing in jail. In January, Debs was sentenced to four years in prison for the Hobbs Act violation. Ultimately, Debs pleaded guilty and was sentenced to fifteen to thirty years in prison on the sex charge. Debs remained in prison until he died of natural causes.

Debs never admitted his involvement in the shooting of Jesse Gray, and the shooter(s) were never identified. But thanks to the Hobbs Act, at least as far as Debs was concerned, justice was served.

16

THEY SHOOT HORSES, DON'T THEY?

In the late fall of 1988, Michigan football coach Bo Schembechler asked me to come to his office. Since 1982, at Bo's request, I had been making annual presentations to Michigan football teams about sports gambling, drugs and violence against women (chapter 7). But at this meeting, Bo and Mike Gittleson, the Michigan strength and conditioning coach, wanted to discuss their concerns about the use of anabolic steroids by football players. (Anabolic refers to a substance that promotes growth. Although all steroids are not anabolic, for simplicity, I will just use the term steroids.)

Several things in 1988 precipitated their concern, including the size and dominance of one of Michigan State's offensive tackles, Tony Mandarich. (*Sports Illustrated* had dubbed Mandarich the "Incredible Bulk" and featured him on the cover of the magazine.) Bo and Gittleson had also learned of a "blind" test for steroids that had been administered to the two teams that were competing in the 1988 Rose Bowl on January 1, 1988: Michigan State and the University of Southern California. Twenty-two Michigan State players had tested positive for steroids. Because the test was blind, it was not known which players tested positive. Although it was suspected that Mandarich was using steroids, it was not until years later that he admitted to using steroids while playing for Michigan State. But it was not just college players who were using. The coaches told me that even some high school players they were seeing in Michigan summer instructional camps were asking, not whether they should use steroids, but when they should start using them.

Bo knew the sale and possession of nonprescription steroids had recently been made a felony under federal law. He wanted to know what was being done to enforce the law. I told him I didn't know but would find out. I also needed to learn more about steroids. Gittleson provided me with some reading material. (Later, Gittleson acted as a consultant when we were getting our case started.)

Steroids are a synthetic version of the male hormone testosterone. When taken orally or intravenously, steroids will, in conjunction with weight training, promote extraordinary weight gain and muscular development. Steroids have become especially prevalent as performance-enhancing drugs (PED) in bodybuilding, professional wrestling, track and field, football, baseball and swimming—really any sport in which strength is a factor. One bodybuilder told me, "To appear in the nationals [the National Body Building Championships] without using steroids would be like competing in the Miss America contest without makeup."

Taken over time, steroids can have detrimental effects on the body, especially when taken at the levels necessary to gain a competitive advantage. Men who take steroids may suffer from hypertension, sterility, female breast development, premature hair loss, infections, cysts or irreversible heart and/or liver damage. Studies also indicate that steroid use increases the risk of developing cancer. Further, prolonged use of steroids may result in the body discontinuing the natural production of testosterone, a condition that could become permanent. Because women, by nature, have little testosterone, steroids pose an even greater threat to them. In addition to most of the problems noted for men, women may develop many masculine traits, such as increased body and facial hair and a deepened voice.

Though athletes may benefit from some aggression behavior brought on by steroid use, it can be difficult to control and can result in socially unacceptable behavior that could be dangerous to the user and others—so-called roid rage. During our investigation, we learned that some police officers were using steroids in conjunction with their strength training. This raised concerns about instances of excessive force by police possibly being attributable to the offending officer(s) exhibiting roid rage. While I was learning about steroids, an FBI agent's son committed suicide because of severe depression caused by his use and cycling off of steroids. Common steroid regimes call for taking steroids over a period then cycling off. During the off cycle, there is a dramatic reduction of testosterone, and the user can become depressed. This made me think about my own daughter and son, who, at the time, were beginning to participate in sports.

Would they be faced with the choice of having to use steroids to reach their athletic goals?

What I found after talking to Bo and Gittleson was that nothing was being done to enforce the federal steroid trafficking statutes. So, I pitched an idea to the drug unit at FBI headquarters in Washington, D.C., to approve a limited undercover operation (UCO) targeting steroid trafficking. They were less than enthusiastic. The drug unit had prioritized investigations of cocaine and heroin dealers. They did not perceive steroid trafficking to be a significant problem. Ultimately, I got approval from a unit that investigates fraud against the government. I argued that steroid dealers were circumventing FDA regulations that defined steroids as prescription drugs. FBIHQ reluctantly authorized a limited UCO. So, our case started out as a low-level undercover investigation with a limited budget and a six-month time limit. Ordinarily, this type of operation can be extended if it is successful, but I was told when our operation was approved that there would be no extension.

From the very beginning, there was a reluctance to pursue the case. FBI administrators and Department of Justice prosecutors did not view steroids as a serious problem. There was an exception, however: Mike Leibson, an assistant U.S. attorney (AUSA) in Detroit. Leibson understood the severity of the problem and not only authorized our investigation but also supported it for five years—all the way to the end of the prosecution phase.

With headquarters's approval and the support of AUSA Leibson, I could begin the UCO. I had asked Bill Randall, a fellow SWAT team member who arrested Loonsfoot (chapter 13) with me, to be the primary undercover agent (UCA). Randall was an experienced "lifter" who knew his way around a weight room. He also had experience as an undercover agent. (The bureau has learned to be careful about who is assigned to work undercover. UCAs receive training but are also psychologically evaluated to determine whether or not they can handle the stress of being in an environment where they are on their own, having to pretend they are criminals.)

Because some dealers were selling veterinary steroids intended to be used on horses, I code named the undercover operation Equine. Equine started slowly. A large obstacle was our lack of an intelligence base. Agents from the Food and Drug Administration (FDA) provided us with some intelligence throughout the investigation and tested some of the steroids we either bought or seized. (Dennis Degan and Dave Kaszubski from the FDA were pioneers in recognizing the serious adverse impact of steroids and human growth hormone.) The steroid black market is a unique culture that is not easily penetrated. Mike Gittleson knew some of the gyms where he had heard steroids were being trafficked. So, Bill Randall got memberships at those gyms. But to be accepted as a fellow "gym rat," you had to frequent the gyms regularly and demonstrate that you were a serious lifter. We developed a plausible background for Randall, and used the name Ed Schmid for his undercover identity. Randall/Schmid was older than most of the lifters, so he was not lifting as intensely as he did in his youth. He was living in Chicago, but he traveled to Michigan frequently to conduct market research. This would explain Schmid's absences from the gym. (Chicago is Randall's real hometown, so he was familiar with it.) Schmid was successful in establishing rapport at some of the gyms, and he was able to make some purchases from street-level dealers and users. (Schmid's pitch was that he had used steroids in the past but was, at the time, buying for lifter buddies back in Chicago.)

All of this took time, and our six-month deadline was swiftly approaching. With only weeks left, I got a call from FBIHQ. The bureau had received an inquiry from the White House (George H.W. Bush was the president at the time) regarding steroid investigations. Equine was the only active federal steroid investigation in the United States at the time, so consequently, FBIHQ wanted me to renew the case and upgrade it. After that, we would have a bigger budget and no time limits. What had been envisioned as a local case morphed into an international operation, targeting dealers from all over the United States, Mexico and Canada. The focus was always to identify and prosecute the largest suppliers.

Those earlier gym rat dealers were confronted and offered favorable treatment if they would identify their suppliers and, in some cases, introduce the UCA to the supplier. (As a matter of policy, we did not prosecute steroid users, only dealers.) Some of the low- or mid-level dealers were athletes or body builders, but none of them had much notoriety, with the exception of then–Mr. Ohio, a body builder.

We worked extensively with the Royal Canadian Mounted Police. One of the Canadian dealers we bought from was supplied by a group that was smuggling steroids into Canada from Europe. The dealer who sold to us was put under surveillance by the Mounties in Ottawa. This led to the arrest of the smugglers and the largest-ever seizure of steroids in Canada.

One of the subjects we prosecuted was Curtis Wenzlaff, who was a supplier to several major-league baseball players. Wenzlaff was living in Oakland, California, at the time and had supplied José Canseco and Mark McGwire, the "Bash Brothers," when they played for the Oakland A's. We never

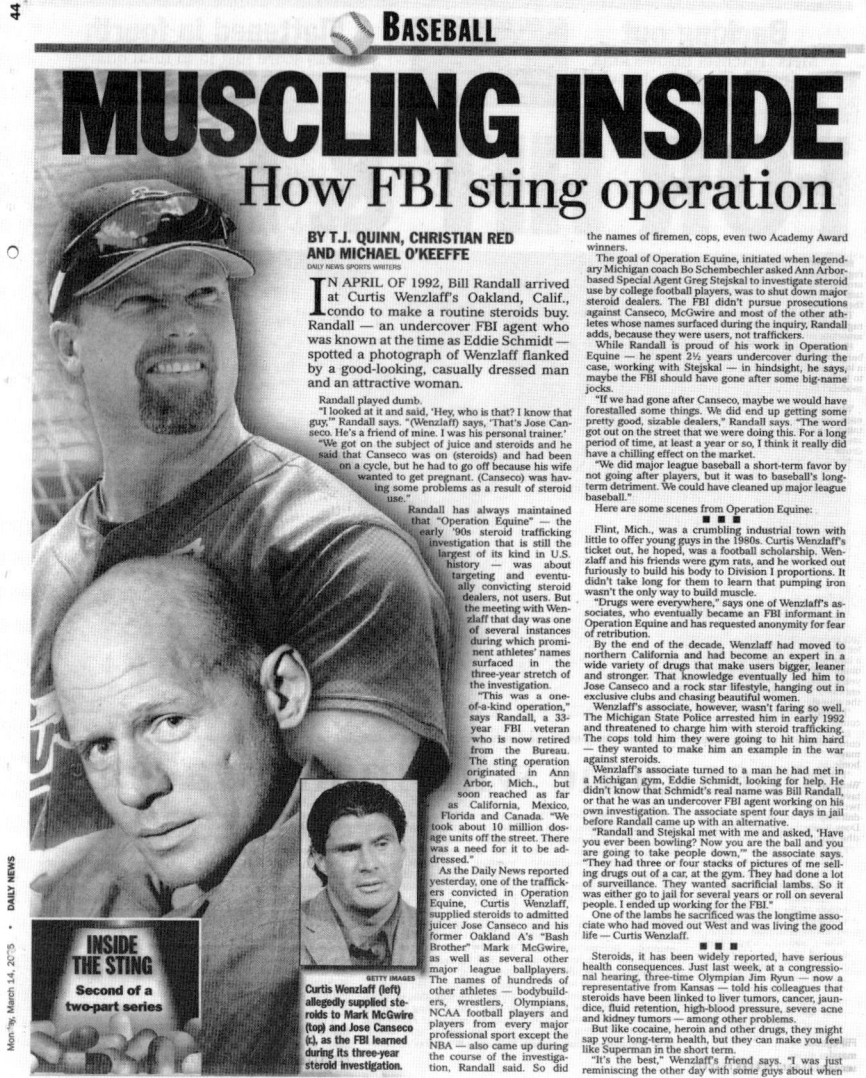

Above and opposite: Feature story about Operation Equine. These images were originally published side-by-side in the *New York Daily News*. The headline ran horizontally across both pages. *Courtesy of* New York Daily News.

prosecuted players unless they were also dealers. Players are just high-profile users—although prosecuting players would probably have generated more publicity for the case. Wenzlaff not only supplied them, but he counseled them which steroids to take and in what amounts as well. Later, Wenzlaff gave us a copy of the steroid regimen he had made up for McGwire. (I

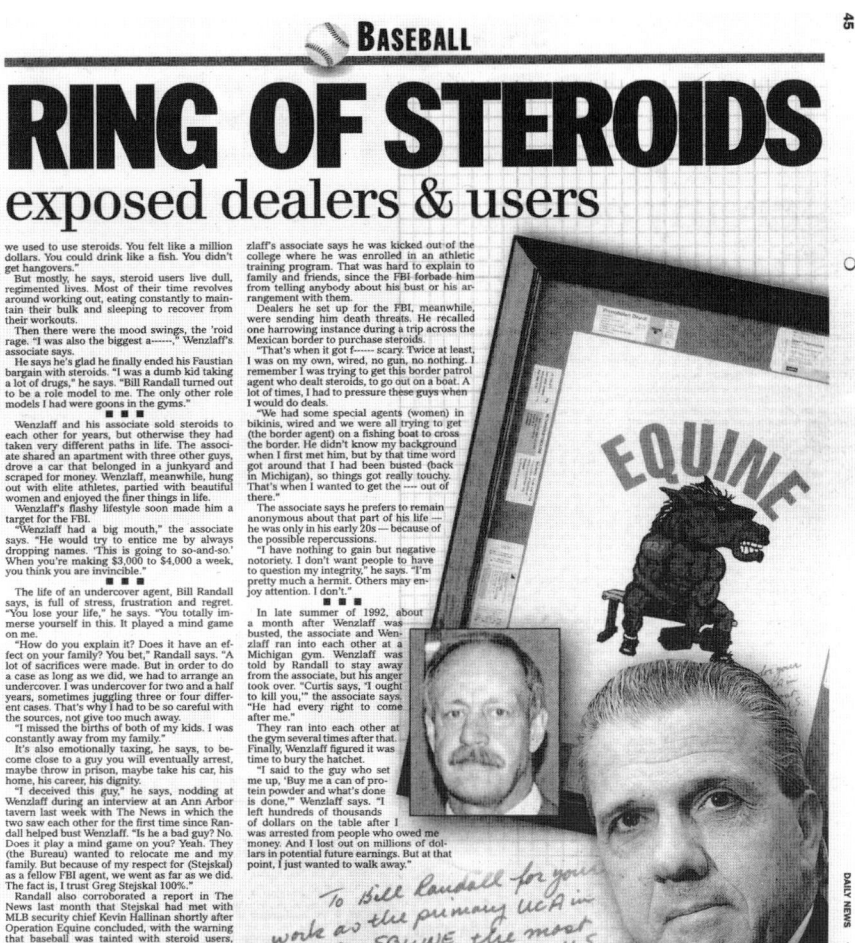

showed that regimen to a veterinarian who told me it was more steroids than he would give to a horse that weighed 1,500 pounds.)

In addition to the UCO, we used a court-authorized telephone wiretap to make a prosecutable case against one exceptionally large dealer and several of his subdealers. We had been unable to penetrate his organization using Ed Schmid. (On the wiretap, we intercepted one conversation in which the dealer threatened to "get rid" of Schmid.) That wiretap allowed us to identify the entire organization and its sources of supply and to intercept a huge shipment of steroids from Mexico. We charged that dealer with a "continuing criminal enterprise," the drug trafficking equivalent of a RICO charge. Because of the potential for a long prison sentence, the CCE dealer identified his suppliers and provided information that led to the solving of a steroid-related homicide.

Operation Equine resulted in conviction of over seventy dealers in several jurisdictions. One convicted dealer had supplied some of the players on that Michigan State team that had raised the concerns of Bo and Gittleson. Ultimately, Equine was successful far beyond our expectations not only with the many convictions of dealers, all of whom pleaded guilty rather than go to trial, but also with seizure of massive amounts of steroids. The Food and Drug Administration estimated that Operation Equine resulted in the seizure of eight to ten million dosage units of real and counterfeit steroids.

Warning Major League Baseball About Steroid Use

In August 1994, I attended a conference at the FBI Academy in Quantico, Virginia, for agents and league officials to making presentations to collegiate and professional sports teams about sports gambling and other issues. Representatives from the NCAA, NFL, MLB, NBA and NHL were also there. I had just written an article for the *FBI Law Enforcement Bulletin*, a magazine that is circulated to police departments nationwide. The article was about the challenges to law enforcement posed by steroid trafficking. The article was given to all the attendees at the conference.

Later, in the Board Room, a restaurant bar at the academy, I talked to Kevin Hallinan. Hallinan was the head of security for the MLB. We talked about steroids and sports. I told him that one of the dealers in our steroid case had supplied Jose Canseco and other MLB players, and the dealer believed that steroid use was pervasive. Hallinan indicated that he was aware that there was a steroid problem in the MLB, but because the players association would not allow testing, there was little the MLB could do about the problem. (At that time, the players were on strike, which was probably also a factor in them not wanting to pursue the issue.) I told Hallinan the FBI would be willing to investigate any dealers who were identified as supplying players, but I never received any information about suspected dealers from MLB.

In 2002, after the Equine case was closed, I arranged, through Hallinan, for his MLB people to interview Curtis Wenzlaff. In the summer of 2004, a Senate subcommittee chaired by Senators Charles Grassley and Joseph Biden held a hearing regarding the prevalence of steroids in sports. I had helped arrange for one of the witnesses to testify at that hearing. The witness, Curtis Wenzlaff, the supplier of Jose Canseco and Mark McGwire, testified that he had supplied steroids to MLB players and said that he was aware that steroid use by MLB players was prevalent. After the hearing, Christian Redd, an investigative reporter for the *New York Daily News*, interviewed Wenzlaff. Redd asked him if he had revealed to the FBI that he had supplied MLB players. Wenzlaff said that he had told an FBI agent, Greg Stejskal.

In February 2005, Jose Canseco went public, admitting to his own steroid use and that of several other MLB players. After Canseco's revelations, I was contacted by Redd and T.J. Quinn, also from the *New York Daily News* (in addition to Redd and Quinn, the *New York Daily News*'s sports investigative team included Terri Thompson and Mike O'Keefe), who asked if I had ever contacted the MLB regarding Wenzlaff's information about supplying MLB players. Ordinarily, if an FBI agent is contacted by the media relating to this kind of information, you would respond with, "No comment." But I knew if I were to say "no comment," it would have implied that we had not warned the MLB. So, I said that we had warned them and told them that I had told Kevin Hallinan about what we had learned during our investigation. I suspected there might be some blowback on this, so after talking to Redd and Quinn, I called Hallinan and left him a voicemail. I never heard from Hallinan, but the following day, my statement was on the front page of the *New York Daily News*, and the story was picked up nationwide.

The MLB denied that I had had ever warned them, and Hallinan denied that he even knew me. The story developed into a major brouhaha. I was instructed by the FBI director's office to make no further comment. Around the same time, I received a phone call from Mike Wallace. I gave Wallace some information "on background" but politely declined his invitation to appear on *60 Minutes*.

Eventually, the MLB did admit that I probably had told them about their steroid problem. (In the 2007 *Mitchell Report* that was commissioned by the MLB to address the proliferation of PEDs, particularly steroids in baseball, one of the report's conclusions was that the FBI had warned the MLB in 1994.) I was never concerned by the MLB's attacks on my veracity, and many people came to my defense, including Bo Schembechler. I was, however, concerned

Cover of *New York Daily News* (2005), reporting that the MLB knew about players' steroid use as early as 1994. *Courtesy of* New York Daily News.

about the irreparable damage that was done to baseball during the so-called steroid era and wished the MLB had acted on my warning.

Later, in 2005, players and MLB officials were called before Congress. Mark McGwire testified at the Congressional hearing but evaded the question of whether or not he had used steroids. Ultimately, McGwire admitted to his extensive and long-term use of steroids, including during a period when he and fellow steroid users Sammy Sosa and Barry Bonds all broke Roger Maris's single-season record for home runs. The 1990s and early 2000s were remembered as the steroid era in baseball—a dark time for America's pastime.

To baseball's credit, the MLB has taken a more aggressive approach against PEDs. Its 2012–13 investigation of Biogenesis, a Florida steroid supplier, resulted in the suspension of fourteen players, including Alex Rodriguez.

I also believe that Bo Schembechler and Mike Gittleson should be recognized for standing up to condemn steroids. When others were ignoring the problem or even tacitly approving steroid use because it gave a competitive advantage, they understood it was an existential threat to the integrity of competitive sports.

17

IS IT OK TO SHOUT FIRE IN A CROWDED CHAT ROOM?

A Michigan Case that Tested Free Speech in the Early Days of the Internet

Free speech has limits, as a famous Supreme Court example illustrates. "Falsely shouting fire in a theater" is not constitutionally protected speech, Justice Oliver Wendell Holmes wrote in 1919. Nearly eight decades later, the first criminal prosecution of threats on the internet again tested the boundary of free speech. I was the case agent in that 1995 landmark case, *United States v. Alkhabaz*.

The defendant was a twenty-year-old University of Michigan student who shortened his name to Jake Baker, rather than use Abraham Jacob Alkhabaz. He was described as quiet and nice and wrote stories with innocent titles, like "Going for a Walk." But he harbored demons. The stories were lurid, graphic tales of kidnapping, raping, torturing and killing young women—so-called snuff stories. Jake posted them at alt.sex.stories, a Usenet chat group, when the internet was still in its infancy. His case raised issues we had not yet faced.

We still face the tricky, high-stakes questions: Where does freedom of speech end, and when does it become a crime? How do you predict when hateful or misogynistic speech will morph into violence? Is it a crime to threaten violence?

Back then, few people knew of the internet. Baker's writings were discovered, thanks to a Michigan alumnus who happened to be in Russia. He stumbled across one of Jake's stories and knew from the IP address that Jake had some UM affiliation. The story used the name of a real Michigan coed as a victim. (In court papers and media accounts, she was referred to as

Jane Doe.) The real Jane was not aware of her characterization in the story or that she was about to be a player in a First Amendment controversy.

The alum contacted university officials, who notified the campus department of public safety (DPS). Detectives from DPS contacted the Washtenaw County prosecutor regarding the online stories. The prosecutor told campus police there was no state criminal statute applicable to Baker's activities. The DPS detectives then contacted the FBI. I read the stories and thought they might constitute a threat, and I was able to get a search warrant for Baker's dormitory room and email account. But the federal magistrate who signed the warrant limited the scope of the warrant to materials and communications related to Baker's "snuff" stories.

Baker lived in the East Quadrangle Dormitory, which also had housed future Unabomber, Ted Kaczynski, during the mid-1960s. The search revealed several more snuff stories by Baker. Two of them used Jane Doe's name, and one contained her address and phone number. One story used Jane Doe's last name in the title of the story. A paragraph in that story achieved notoriety, as it appeared often in the print media. "As an introduction to his stories, Baker wrote: 'Torture is foreplay. Rape is romance. Snuff is climax.'" This is an excerpt from that story:

> *Then Jerry and I tie her by her long brown hair to the ceiling fan, so that she is dangling midair. Her feet don't touch the ground. She kicks trying to hit me, Jerry or the gorund [sic]. The sight of her wiggling in mid-air, hands rudely taped behind her back, turns me on. Jerry takes a big spiky hairbrush and starts beating her small breasts with it, coloring them with nice red marks. She screams and struggles harder.*

At this point, the story goes from R-rated to X-rated. It ends with Baker's protagonist lighting Jane Doe on fire.

The search of his email account revealed numerous messages between Jake and an individual identifying himself as Arthur Gonda, believed to be residing in Ontario, Canada. In these messages, Jake and Gonda discuss actually getting together and committing the acts Jake had depicted. This is part of a December 1994 email from Jake to Gonda:

> *I've started doing is going back and rereading earlier messages of yours. Each time I do, they turn me on more and more. I can't wait to see you in person. I've been trying to think of secluded spots, but my area knowledge of Ann Arbor is limited to the campus. I don't want any blood in my*

> room, though I've come upon an excellent method to abduct a bitch—As I said before, my room is right across from the girl's bathroom. Wiat [sic] until late at night, grab her when she goes to unlock the door. Knock her unconscious and put her into one of those portable lockers (forgot the word for it), or even a duffle bag. Then hurry her out to the car and take her away...what do you think?

This was Gonda's response:

> Hi Jake. I have been out tonight and I can tell you that I am thinking more and more about "doing" a girl. I can picture it so well...and I can think of no better use of their flesh. I HAVE to make a bitch suffer!

Baker's response, in part:

> I know how you feel. I've been masturbating like the devil recently. Just thinking about it anymore doesn't do the trick...I need TO DO IT.

After reading Jake's stories and emails, I concluded that the electronic messages, in context with the stories, constituted a threat as defined by a federal statute (18 USC § 875[c]) that deals with transmitting "in interstate or foreign commerce any communication containing any threat to kidnap any person or to injure any person." The statute was written in 1948, long before the internet, but the internet was clearly an instrument of interstate commerce. I presented the case to the Detroit U.S. attorney's office, which agreed with my conclusion. Our contention was that Jake had threatened not only Jane Doe, but all coeds in East Quadrangle.

Jake was arrested on a complaint and warrant and arraigned before a federal magistrate in Detroit. We did not request detention, but after reading some of Jake's literary works, the magistrate felt he was dangerous and ordered him kept in custody.

The case was assigned to U.S. District Court Judge Avern Cohn. It was apparent that Judge Cohn was not a fan of the government's case. He made it clear that Jake's stories were protected by the First Amendment's free speech clause and could not be part of the prosecution. So, when Jake was indicted, all references to the stories were eliminated. (I argued against dropping the stories, as I believed Cohn would toss the case no matter what we did. In addition to providing context, the stories named a potential victim with her actual address.) Cohn did dismiss the indictment, saying Jake's emails were nothing more than a

FBI Case Files Michigan

THE NEW YORK TIMES, SATURDAY, FEBRUARY 11, 1995

An Internet Author of Sexually Violent Fiction Faces Charges

By PETER H. LEWIS

A University of Michigan student who was jailed for publishing a sexually violent work of fiction about a classmate on the global Internet computer network was denied bail yesterday.

Magistrate Thomas A. Carlson of Federal District Court in Detroit said that although the 20-year-old Abraham Jacob Alkhabaz, who uses the name Jake Baker, had never physically approached or spoken with the classmate, the writing suggested that Mr. Baker was "disturbed" and "dangerous," and that he was "a ticking time bomb waiting to go off."

Mr. Baker, a sophomore from Boardman, Ohio, was arrested in Ann Arbor, Mich., by agents of the Federal Bureau of Investigation on Thursday and charged with the Federal crime of transporting threatening material across state lines. If convicted, he faces a maximum penalty of five years in prison.

The incident is the latest in a series of cases involving computer networks in which law-enforcement authorities in the United States have tried to apply existing laws to the new and uncharted domain of cyberspace.

Mr. Baker was suspended from the university last week, three weeks after he used a school computer to write and electronically publish a story on an electronic forum that specializes in sexually explicit fiction. Before he was taken to jail, Mr. Baker told reporters that his story was protected by First Amendment guarantees of free speech.

In his story, "Pamela's Ordeal," Mr. Baker used the name of a female student who had been in one of his classes last semester, as the object of violent sexual fantasies.

He posted the story on "alt.sex.stories," one of the most popular of the thousands of forums, known as news groups, that make up Usenet, an international network. Mr. Baker added a note to the story indicating that it was "sick stuff," and that he had never spoken to the woman whose name he used in the story.

The Michigan Daily newspaper reported that Mr. Baker's story involved "torturing a woman with a hot curling iron, and mutilating and sodomizing her while she is gagged to a chair."

A University of Michigan alumnus in Moscow was browsing the alt.sex.stories news group in Russia, saw the story, noted its origin and alerted school officials. Campus police and Federal agents were asked to investigate.

In an affidavit filed in the case, an F.B.I. agent, Greg Stejskal, said that in addition to filing his story, Mr. Baker had an electronic exchange of messages with subscribers to alt.sex.stories in which Mr. Baker described his "desire to commit acts of abduction, bondage, torture, mutilation, sodomy, rape and murder of young women."

"This young man posted it into a Usenet group that had other similar postings," said Andrew Taubman, executive director of the Electronic Freedom Foundation, a lobbying group in Washington. "They accepted it as a type of writing that was acceptable under their community standards."

The group known as alt.sex.stories is among the hundreds of groups known as "unmoderated." Anyone with access to the forums, which are commonly reached through the Internet, can post material there.

The president of the university, James J. Duderstadt, suspended Mr. Baker on Feb. 1, citing school bylaws that give the president the power to maintain "health, diligence and order among the students."

The arrest and jailing of Mr. Baker was criticized by several groups, including the American Civil Liberties Union and the university's Student Civil Liberties Watch.

"It's part of a fairly long series of cases in which the authorities have tried to stretch existing laws into areas where they are not particularly applicable," said David Banisar, a lawyer for the Electronic Privacy Information Center in Washington.

A student's story raises issues of free speech in cyberspace.

"Idle banter across the Internet, even if it is discussing things most people are appalled by, is still not a crime, any more than if it were discussed in a bar or a college dormitory."

"The Internet doesn't have state lines," Mr. Taubman said. "It is arguable that the Internet doesn't even have national boundaries."

The female student whose name Mr. Baker used, identified in court papers as "Jane Doe," reportedly was not aware of the story until she was contacted by reporters.

David Cahill, Mr. Baker's lawyer, said the story was never meant as a threat.

"At the hearing, a psychologist and a psychiatrist both testified that Jake is not dangerous to himself or others," Mr. Cahill said. "It was a fictional story, written in the present tense. It was not in the future tense, and nothing in the story identified the woman as a University of Michigan student."

Mr. Cahill said his client "seemed to be holding up relatively well."

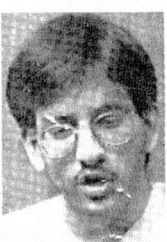

Abraham Jacob Alkhabaz, who uses the name Jake Baker.

New York Times's coverage of Jake Baker (photograph) case, the first prosecution of an internet threat (1995). *Courtesy of the* New York Times.

Detroit Free Press

On Guard For 164 Years

Metro Final
Partly cloudy, humid.
High 86. Low 65.
Friday: Partly cloudy, warmer.

Thursday
June 22, 1995
35 cents (50 cents outside 6-county metropolitan area)
For home delivery call 1-313-222-6500

Internet author's charges dismissed

Judge criticizes prosecutors in U-M case

BY JIM SCHAEFER AND MARYANNE GEORGE
Free Press Staff Writers

Jake Baker was charged with transmitting threats after posting a rape story about a student.

A federal judge in Detroit on Wednesday tossed out criminal charges against Internet rape story author Jake Baker, saying the government had butted into what should have remained a University of Michigan disciplinary case.

U.S. District Judge Avern Cohn called Baker's jailing for 29 days earlier this year "disturbing" and "inexplicable," saying three psychological evaluations done before the FBI arrested him showed no potential for violence.

Cohn also slammed government prosecutors, saying they tried to salvage a case they knew could not be won.

The judge's ruling followed a monthlong hearing in five charges of transmitting threats be dismissed because Baker's violent Internet writings were protected as free speech. The government had argued that true threats are not protected.

Cohn also slammed government prosecutors, saying they tried to salvage a case they knew could not be won.

A man who answered the phone at Baker's Ohio residence said of Cohn's decision, "We're going to read it thoroughly. Jake is not going to say anything until after we have had a chance to go over it... We will have something to say later."

U.S. Attorney Saul Green issued a terse response to Cohn's ruling, saying his office's push to prosecute Baker was "absolutely" worthwhile.

"We strongly disagree with the court's reasoning in the decision," said Green, who at one point had a team of prosecutors making recommendations on the case. He said he will decide in a week or two whether to request permission from his superiors to appeal.

The lead FBI agent, Greg Stejskal,

said Cohn's decision that Baker's writings lacked intent made him worry.

"As a husband and a father of a daughter, it looks like a threat to me," Stejskal said.

Susan McGee, executive director of the Domestic Violence Project in Washtenaw County, said the ruling "shows the judicial system in the United States is more interested in men's rights to torture, beat and harass women than it is in women's right to live their lives in peace and safety."

See BAKER, Page 7A

Front page—banner headline, Jake Baker's charges dismissed. *Courtesy of the* Detroit Free Press.

private conversation discussing fantasies and were thus protected as free speech. He criticized the government and its "overzealous agent," referring to me.

The government appealed to the Sixth Circuit Court of Appeals in Cincinati. A 2–1 decision by that court said the emails did not constitute a threat because they were "not conveyed to effect some change or achieve some goal through intimidation." The dissenting judge pointed out—correctly, I think—that if Congress intended proof of such an intent, it would have said so. (The appellate judges could not consider the emails in context with the gruesome stories, as the stories were not part of the indictment.)

I don't know where Jake is now, and I have no reason to believe he ever tried to bring his horrific fantasies to life—but he might have had we not interceded. (He spent thirty days in the U.S. Marshal's detention facility before Cohn tossed the indictment.)

Troubling Precedent

In an age of terrorism, both domestic and international, law enforcement is left with the conundrum of how to address internet communications that could be preparation for criminal acts. Most mass shootings have been preceded by internet postings from the shooters. The alleged El Paso shooter, who killed twenty-two people on August 3, 2019, posted a White nationalist screed, saying, in part: "This attack is a response to the Hispanic invasion of Texas. They are the instigators not me. I am simply defending my country from the cultural and ethnic replacement brought on by the invasion." His Walmart murders occurred minutes after the posting. But if no attack occurred, would the screed constitute a criminal threat that could be prosecuted?

In its effort to combat domestic terrorism, the FBI now pays more attention to social media—including chat rooms and sites frequented by white nationalists, as well as sites where misogynistic messages are shared. In 1995, we may have been on to something but didn't know it. Misogyny, the professed hatred of women and or violent acts against women, was a common characteristic of shooters in more than half of U.S. mass shootings from 2009 to 2017. Analysts who monitor these sites are developing profiles of potential mass shooters based on their posts. Their findings, coupled with stricter background checks and a federal red flag law, would not eliminate all mass shootings, but it would stop some.

A recent example is the June 2019 arrest of Ross Farca, age twenty-three, by police in Concord, California, based on FBI information. Farca had allegedly made online threats to carry out a mass shooting at a synagogue. He had written, in part, "I would probably get a body count of like 30 k———s (an ethnic slur for Jews) and then like five police officers because I would also decide to fight to the death." No date, time or specific synagogue was identified, but this alleged threat led to a search warrant being executed at Farca's residence, where police found an illegally modified AR-15, thirty high-capacity magazines and Nazi literature. Farca was charged with making criminal threats and possessing an illegal assault rifle. He is, at the time of this writing, out on $125,000 bail to await trial.

Perhaps this was a mass shooting that did not occur because of better vigilance of the internet and a better understanding of what constitutes a threat.

18

THE HISTORY OF APRIL 19

American Revolution, Waco and the Oklahoma City Bombing

> *Listen my children, and you shall hear*
> *Of the midnight ride of Paul Revere,*
> *On the eighteenth of April, in Seventy Five....*
> —*"Paul Revere's Ride," Henry Wadsworth Longfellow*

Longfellow's poem forever immortalized Paul Revere's ride, but what it does not say is that Revere's mission that night was to warn Samuel Adams and John Hancock that British soldiers were coming to Lexington to arrest them. It was after midnight on April 19 when Revere arrived in Lexington and warned Adams and Hancock. Revere also aroused the countryside, and that morning, the minutemen met the British regulars on Lexington Green. No one knows who fired the first shot—"the shot heard around the world." But on that morning, April 19, 1775, the American Revolution began.

In a perverse twist of fate, April 19, 1993, was the fifty-first day of a siege at the Branch Davidian Compound, also known as Mount Carmel, outside of Waco, Texas. It was to be the last day of the siege, a culmination of a series of bad decisions and missed opportunities.

The siege began on February 28. The Bureau of Alcohol, Tobacco and Firearms (ATF) had gone to the Davidian Compound to execute search warrants. The warrants were based on affidavits stating that the Davidians possessed certain illegal weapons, including fully automatic weapons and components to convert semiautomatic weapons into fully automatic weapons. Some of the Davidians were known to have a propensity for violence, including their leader, David Koresh, who had changed his name from Vernon Howell. There had been a power struggle a few years earlier within the Branch Davidians, and a gunfight had ensued. The history of the Branch Davidians and how they ended up in Waco, led by Koresh, is a long story that won't be told here. Suffice it to say, Koresh became the leader and subsequently claimed to be a messiah who could procreate with any of his women followers, irrespective of their age or marital status. The group had embraced an apocalyptic philosophy, which relied heavily on the book of Revelation in the Bible.

The ATF had been surveilling the compound from a home across the road for several weeks prior to the raid. They had also placed an undercover (UC) agent within the Davidians. However, the surveillance was compromised, and at some point, Koresh learned of the UC agent. In addition, one of the Davidians was also the local postman. On the morning of the ATF raid, a TV crew asked the postman for directions to the compound, as they had learned there was to be a raid. The postman gave them directions and took the news of the impending raid back to the compound.

The ATF was aware of the Davidians' potential for violence and obviously knew they had a large stockpile of firearms and ammunition. Consequently, the element of surprise was an important aspect of their raid plan. However, surprise was an early casualty. ATF's leadership was aware their plan had been compromised but chose to proceed anyway.

The ATF agents were met at the front door of the compound by Koresh and some of his "mighty men" (that's how Koresh referred to his young male followers). There was a short standoff, and then someone opened fire. It has never been determined who fired the first shot; both sides claim it was the other. Whoever fired, it escalated into a gun battle, resulting in the deaths of four ATF agents (sixteen wounded) and six Davidians. Koresh was wounded, along with several of his followers. Thus began the siege of the Branch Davidian Compound.

The FBI was given control of the siege. Negotiations between the Davidians and the FBI began and continued throughout the siege. Although the FBI was thrust into a situation not of its own making, it learned valuable lessons. Unfortunately, many of the lessons were learned through making mistakes.

Ultimately, it became clear that Koresh was not negotiating in good faith. Koresh had said that he would surrender but that he needed to finish his own scripture, something he called the "Seven Seals." But surreptitiously placed microphones inside the compound picked up conversations indicating that Koresh was stalling and did not intend to surrender.

The FBI, with the concurrence of Attorney General Reno and President Clinton, decided to pressure Koresh and his followers into surrender by punching holes into the compound walls and injecting tear gas. The conventional way to place tear gas is to fire projectiles containing tear gas into the targeted area. These projectiles explode on impact and expel tear gas, but this process also produces heat, which can result in fire. The method devised for the compound entailed the use of converted tanks to spray the tear gas directly into the holes made in the walls. The error was not in how the tear gas was injected, but rather, in underestimating the potential for mass suicide of an apocalyptic cult. The FBI was warned of this potential, but it was discounted. After all, what person would choose suicide over surrender, not only for themselves, but for their children?

Then there were the fires that ultimately consumed the entire compound. Although a Congressional investigation determined that the fires had been set by the Davidians, the anti-government and conspiracy-minded will forever believe that they were set or caused by the government. Seventy-six Davidians, including Koresh, died that day, and at least twenty of them were killed by self-inflicted gunshot wounds or consensual execution (suicide by proxy). Nine people escaped from the fire, and presumably others could have done the same if they had wanted to. (One woman ran out of the compound and was tackled by an FBI agent in order to keep her from going back.)

Timothy McVeigh, the Oklahoma City bomber, witnessed part of the siege. McVeigh was sympathetic to the Davidians and was outraged that the siege ended in the conflagration and death of Koresh and most of his followers. It is not clear when McVeigh's anti-government beliefs began, but those beliefs were growing and becoming an obsession. It is difficult to encapsulate McVeigh's philosophy. It was clearly anti-government and became vehemently so; it was an amalgamation of White supremacy, anti-Semitism and fear of a "New World Order," that is, a belief in a worldwide conspiracy to take over the world and the U.S. government's leadership being in league with this conspiracy. If there was an overriding theme in McVeigh's beliefs, it was probably that he was trying to replicate the plot of *The Turner Diaries*, a 1978 novel written by William Luther Piece (a White supremacist) under the pseudonym Andrew MacDonald. The book depicts a violent revolution in the United States, ignited by the bombing of the FBI headquarters, which leads to the overthrow of the U.S. government, nuclear war and, ultimately, a race war that results in the extermination of all Jews and non-Whites.

While in the military, McVeigh met Terry Nichols. They became friends, and their friendship continued after they left the military. Nichols was a follower and embraced McVeigh's philosophy and paranoia. After the Davidian Compound siege ended, McVeigh began to develop a plan to destroy a federal building—an act of retaliation for what had occurred in Waco. Initially, the plan was to destroy the building when it was unoccupied, but McVeigh decided that he needed to send a stronger message, and that would require people to die. Later, McVeigh would say, "Kids and women are fair game."

McVeigh and Nichols's plan coalesced into the selection of the Alfred P. Murrah Federal Building in Oklahoma City as the target. The plan was to build a bomb and place it in the back of a truck. McVeigh and Nichols researched how to construct a large bomb and experimented with making and detonating explosives at the Nichols's farm near Decker, Michigan.

In April 1995, McVeigh, using another name, rented a truck in Junction City, Kansas. McVeigh and Nichols had previously obtained and stored the components for the bomb. In a park outside of Junction City, they assembled the bomb in the back of the rental truck. The bomb consisted of thirteen fifty-five-gallon drums—nine containing ammonium nitrate (fertilizer) and nitromethane (racing fuel) and four containing fertilizer and diesel fuel. Also with the drums was about 350 pounds of Tovex, a commercial explosive. The Tovex would act as primary or initiator. McVeigh ran two fuses from the cargo bay to the cab of the truck. The fuses were attached to blasting caps that would set off the Tovex. The bomb weighed about 4,800 pounds and cost about $5,000.

Prior to April 19, Nichols and McVeigh drove to Oklahoma City and parked the getaway car several blocks from the Murrah Federal Building. They then drove back to Junction City. McVeigh stayed at a motel in Junction City. Although McVeigh used another name when he rented the truck, at the motel, he used his real name with the Decker, Michigan farm as his permanent address.

On April 19, McVeigh drove the bomb-laden truck to Oklahoma City. A few blocks from the federal building, he lit one fuse. Then, just prior to parking the truck at the federal building, he lit the backup fuse. He then exited the truck and ran the few blocks to the getaway car. When the bomb exploded, it did so with the force of five thousand pounds of TNT. It destroyed the federal building, killing 168 people and injuring over 700. It

The Murrah Federal Building after the bombing on April 19, 1995. *FBI photograph.*

also damaged or destroyed 324 other buildings. Among the fatalities were children, as the federal building housed a childcare center on the street level. McVeigh knew about the childcare center.

Within hours, the FBI had identified the rental truck (from the VIN on an axle that had been blown some distance from the site) and knew it had been rented in Junction City. Agents dispatched to Junction City discovered that the truck had been rented under a false name but that the same person used a different name, Timothy McVeigh, at a nearby motel.

A BOL (be on the lookout) bulletin was broadcast, and it was learned McVeigh had been arrested by the Oklahoma State Police for driving a car without a license plate. An alert trooper also saw that McVeigh was carrying a concealed handgun. McVeigh was about to be released, but a hold was placed on him, and FBI agents took him into custody.

Two days later, the FBI went to the Decker farm to execute search warrants. The Detroit FBI SWAT team was sent in first to secure the farm, as there was a concern about armed coconspirators (the extent of the conspiracy was not yet known) and explosives at the farm. I was one of the SWAT team leaders involved. The farm was operated by James Nichols, Terry's brother. It was known James had anti-government sentiments, but there was never sufficient evidence to prosecute him for being involved in the conspiracy or

Left: A Timothy McVeigh photograph and sketch from a witness at a truck rental agency in Junction City, Kansas. *FBI photograph.*

Below: Detroit FBI SWAT team making entry into the farmhouse on James Nichols's farm near Decker, Michigan (April 21, 1995). *Author's collection.*

having knowledge of it. The search of the farm did uncover bomb-making materials and evidence that bombs had been tested there.

McVeigh had picked April 19 for the date of the bombing because it was the 2nd anniversary of the end of the siege at the Davidian Compound. It also happened to be the 220th anniversary of that shot heard around the world. When McVeigh was arrested, he had a quote from Samuel Adams (one of the men Paul Revere was sent to warn): "When the government fears the people, there is liberty. When the people fear the government, there is tyranny." Underneath the quote, McVeigh had scrawled, "Maybe now there will be liberty." McVeigh also had pages from *The Turner Diaries*, the racist and anti-Semitic diatribe masquerading as a novel.

It dishonors our founding fathers when McVeigh and some militias try to cloak themselves in the legitimacy of the men who valiantly fought for our independence and, at the same time, embrace the ideology of the White supremacy movement. It is perverse to equate what our founding fathers did and endured to establish a Constitutional government with the bombing of a federal building that killed 168 people, whose only crime was being in or near that building.

The lesson that was learned on April 19, 1995, was that we in law enforcement—or as citizens—must take the anti-government movements seriously. Their ideology may seem foolish and historically and theologically spurious, but that does not diminish their potential for harm.

19

THE TALE OF THE STOLEN METEORITE

Almost an X-File

In the Ann Arbor RA, we were primarily responsible for investigating violations of federal law in five counties that had a total population of about one million people. Ann Arbor is also the home of the University of Michigan, one of the largest and most prestigious research institutions in the world.

A good thing about working in an RA was there were a variety of cases—some were unique.

It was August 1998 when I got a call from Detective Kevin McNulty of the UM Department of Public Safety. McNulty and I had worked cases together before, and he told me that they had located a meteorite that had been stolen from the UM Museum of Natural History. McNulty explained that the sixty-pound meteorite, worth about $10,000, was stolen from the fourth floor of the museum a few days before.

Apparently, there was good market for meteorites, especially ones from the Canyon Diablo ("devil" in Spanish) Meteor Crater, also known as the Barringer Crater, near Flagstaff, Arizona. That crater has gained a sort of a science-fiction cult fascination with the people who believe extraterrestrials have visited Earth and may be among us. Part of this fascination is probably because the crater is relatively young in Earth's geological history and still looks like an impact crater, like the ones on the moon. (In the 1984 movie *Starman*, the extraterrestrial character played by Jeff Bridges is trying to get to the Barringer Crater to rendezvous with a rescue craft from his home planet.)

Tales of a G-Man

The Canyon Diablo Meteor Crater, near Flagstaff, Arizona. *Courtesy of Google photographs.*

The meteorite that was stolen from the museum was actually a fragment of a much larger meteor that created the crater in Diablo Canyon when it struck the earth about fifty thousand years ago. It is estimated that the meteor weighed about sixty thousand tons, with a diameter of approximately 100 feet, and was traveling at thirty thousand miles per hour when it hit. Most of the meteor vaporized on impact, but pieces of it were strewn around the crater. The impact had the explosive power of a ten-megaton bomb (one megaton is equivalent to one million tons of TNT). The crater is almost 600 feet deep and is about 3,900 feet across.

No humans would have been around to witness the impact. It would be at least ten thousand years before any humans reached the area. It was the Spanish explorers in the sixteenth century who named the canyon Diablo. For reasons that have since been lost, the Natives who descended from the earlier inhabitants considered the canyon cursed.

In the early 1900s, Daniel Barringer, a mining engineer who made millions from silver mining in Arizona, took an interest in the crater. He believed that the crater had been caused by a meteor impact. The prevailing scientific theory at the time was that the crater had resulted from some type of volcanic activity and that the meteorite fragments around the crater were coincidental. But because fragments found in the area were composed of iron and nickel, Barringer believed the main mass of the meteor was buried beneath the floor of the crater and that it was worth millions. Over the next several years, Barringer drilled numerous exploratory holes in the floor of the crater—some as deep as 1,400 feet—but he never hit any main mass, nor did he discover an alien spacecraft.

Barringer rightly deduced that the crater was created by a meteor impact, but he did not understand the physics of the tremendous force caused by the impact that resulted in the near-total vaporization of the meteor, leaving only fragments. The Barringer family still owns the crater. It is a popular tourist attraction and has been designated a national historical site.

Meanwhile, back in Ann Arbor, there were no witnesses to the theft of the meteorite, and at the time, no surveillance cameras were in the area of the theft. After the theft, Detective McNulty put a photograph and description of the meteorite on the internet, a relatively new forum for broadcasting reports of stolen property. A rock dealer named Michael Casper was surfing the internet when he came across McNulty's posting. Casper contacted the UM museum and confirmed that the meteorite he had purchased was the one that had been stolen. McNulty wanted to recover the meteorite but was concerned that Casper, the dealer in New York, might not cooperate. McNulty had no police power in New York.

I agreed to call Casper, and he was very cooperative. He understood that he was in possession of stolen property and that because it had been transported interstate, his continued possession of it was a potential violation of federal law. He agreed to return it to UM. Casper also provided the name and address of the person who had sold the meteorite to him: Steven Collins. Collins had called Casper and told him he had a sixty-pound Diablo Canyon meteorite for sale. Casper initially agreed to purchase it for $2,300. When Collins delivered the meteorite, they agreed that Casper would pay $1,000 and trade a prehistoric crab fossil and a two-hundred-pound slab of crystallized purple quartz, or amethyst, for the meteorite.

Both McNulty and I assumed that the name and address that had been provided to Casper were both false, but it turned out that there was a Steven Collins living at the address in Pittsfield Township, just outside of Ann Arbor. That Steven Collins had been convicted of second-degree murder in Michigan, had served time and was currently on parole, which would provide some leverage when dealing with Collins.

McNulty contacted Collins, and he readily admitted that he had sold the meteorite to the dealer in New York. Collins said he had run into a guy he met in prison, and the guy had offered to sell him a meteorite that he said he found in Arizona. He paid the guy a few hundred dollars, knowing the meteorite was worth much more. Collins claimed he didn't know the meteorite was stolen. Collins gave the name of the inmate, but no one by that name could be found in the records of the Michigan Department of Corrections.

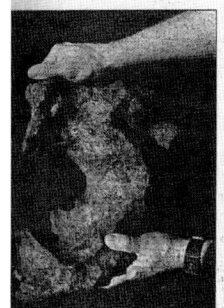

"Meteorite Returned." *Courtesy of the* Ann Arbor *(MI)* News, *October 1, 1998.*

Although McNulty had recovered the meteorite, he did not have enough evidence to prosecute Collins for the theft from the museum. I thought we might be able to prosecute Collins federally for interstate transportation of stolen property (ITSP), but for that, we needed him to admit that he knew the meteorite was stolen. I believed Collins had stolen the meteorite himself, but I was pretty sure he wasn't going to admit to that. However, sometimes a bad denial can be almost as good as a confession.

I wanted to interview Collins again, and I wanted it to be a surprise. I did not want to give him time to prepare, or worse, decide he didn't want to talk to me. I decided to try to talk to him where he worked. At the time, he was working for a construction company testing a cleared and graded site for the level of compaction of the soil—a good job for a self-described rockhound. I told Collins that we were having some trouble with his original story, as there was no inmate by the name he had given us who had ever been in the Michigan Prison System. Collins said that he hadn't bought the meteorite from a former inmate but from a guy he met in bar. He said he couldn't admit to having been in a bar because that was a violation of his parole. (I didn't mention that his having left Michigan and traveling to New York without permission was also a parole violation.) He claimed that, in the bar, he struck up a conversation with a guy about rocks. The guy seemed to be fairly knowledgeable and said he had a meteorite that he wanted to sell. They went to the guy's car, and in the trunk, there was a large meteorite that the guy said had come from Diablo Canyon. Collins knew that it was a meteorite and had some idea of its value. He agreed to buy it for $400. He paid in cash and had no documentation of the sale.

Collins claimed that he didn't know the guy's name, nor did have any contact information for him. Collins hadn't seen him before or since. He also said he hadn't noticed whether the car's license was from out of state. He was only able to give a very general description of the guy. Collins told me the name of the bar but said he didn't know any of the employees or patrons in the bar. He didn't think there was anyone in the bar who could corroborate any part of his story. Collins had not only changed his story when it was challenged, he had provided what I thought was a pretty weak new story as to how he acquired the meteorite—"a bad denial."

Collins was federally charged with interstate transportation of stolen property and his parole violation for having left Michigan. He pleaded guilty and admitted to the judge that he knew the meteorite was stolen when he transported it to New York. He was sentenced to nine months in prison, in addition to the two years for parole violation.

We never did learn how he was able to get the meteorite out of the museum without being seen. But as the saying goes: "The truth is out there."

20

THE HOLE-IN-THE-TRUCK GANG

It was a cold early spring Saturday morning, and I was following a lead in a rural part of Michigan. I had received a call on Friday afternoon that there was a unique piece of evidence on a farm near the Michigan–Ohio border. When I got to the farm, I contacted the owner and identified myself. He walked me to the back of an outbuilding. There, parked in the weeds, was a white cargo van with flat tires. The farmer opened the van's back door. In the middle of the cargo bay was a circular hole that had been cut in the floor.

So, why was I out here on a cold Saturday morning, looking at a van with a hole in its floor?

It all started in the summer the year before, in 1998. An Environmental Protection Agency–FBI task force that was working illegal dumping cases had received information that a waste disposal company near Ann Arbor, Michigan, was defrauding clients by not doing work and overcharging. There were also rumors that the company was surreptitiously creating spills, which it then charged clients to clean up. The information was fragmented, and it was coming primarily from disgruntled employees. The disposal firm in question was Hi-Po, which had been in business for about nine years. The founders, Aaron Smith, who was just twenty-six, and Stephen Carbeck, age thirty-four, had started with a pickup truck and a power washer. They had grown Hi-Po to more than one hundred employees and several vacuum trucks, valued at well over $200,000 each at the time. By all accounts, Hi-Po had become extraordinarily successful, with such clients as the University of Michigan and Chrysler.

In the summer of 1998, however, the EPA-FBI task force learned that, recently, one of the Hi-Po employees had quit because he was reportedly upset with Hi-Po not performing work and then charging for the work that hadn't been done. That employee, Michael Stagg, had retired from the Washtenaw County (Michigan) drain commissioner's office prior to working at Hi-Po. EPA agent Greg Horvath and FBI agent Steve Flattery, both from the task force, and I went to Stagg's home in Ann Arbor. He wasn't surprised to see us and said he had been thinking about coming to us.

Stagg was very forthcoming, but he had only limited direct knowledge. He said he had inspected a Hi-Po clean-up project in Riverview, a city south of Detroit. There, he saw that Hi-Po had done only about half of the work it had been contracted to do, but Stagg was told Hi-Po billed Riverview for the entire job. (Later, we learned that a Riverview official was receiving kickbacks.) Because Stagg had left Hi-Po, he had no ability to get additional evidence. He did suggest, however, that we contact Greg Cainstraight (a good name for a potential cooperating witness), who had been recently hired as Hi-Po's chief financial officer. Stagg seemed to think that Cainstraight was uncomfortable with some of the things Hi-Po was doing and might be cooperative.

Cainstraight had attended West Point and played football there. He later transferred to Michigan State University, where he received his accounting degree. We decided to meet Cainstraight cold and try to get a feel for whether he might be willing to work with us. It was a gamble. We did not have a strong case, and if we approached Cainstraight and he wasn't cooperative, he could go back and warn Smith and Carbeck of the investigation. With forewarning, they could have made it extremely difficult for us to make a case.

I knew it was important to establish some rapport with Cainstraight. I talked to him about playing college football and being a West Point cadet. The West Point motto, "Duty, honor, country," was mentioned in our conversation, as was *The Long Gray Line*, John Ford's movie and Rick Atkinson's book. I think Cainstraight would have been cooperative no matter who had contacted him, but it is important for a cooperating witness to trust the agent who handles him. We did develop a trusting a relationship, and as a result, he agreed to attempt to record possibly incriminating conversations with Smith and Carbeck.

Cainstraight told us that Smith and/or Carbeck would, on occasion, come to his office and discuss business matters. It would not have been practical to have Cainstraight "wired" all the time. (This was before miniature digital recorders were generally available. We were still using NAGRA reel-to-reel tape recorders.) So, we decided to wire Cainstraight's briefcase, which he told us he customarily kept next to his desk. Our tech guys put a recorder in the briefcase and made a small hole for the microphone. They also placed an exterior on/off switch so that Cainstraight could easily activate the recorder.

In September, when I delivered the briefcase to Cainstraight, we talked about recording conversations. We decided to see what transpired without trying to orchestrate any meeting. If that didn't work, we agreed that we might try to instigate something.

Within days, Cainstraight called me and said he thought he had recorded a good conversation. (He had no way to review the tape, as NAGRAs don't have playback capability.) "Good conversation" turned out to be a dramatic understatement. Smith and Carbeck had come to Cainstraight's office and, for about two hours, given a running narrative of their criminal activity at Hi-Po. They talked about defrauding the University of Michigan—how they billed UM for whole days of sewer maintenance, even though Hi-Po was doing nothing. On jobs where Hi-Po was doing work for UM and other clients, they substantially over-billed. They even alluded to employees at UM, Chrysler and Riverview who they were bribing to play along.

But most disturbing were their stories of the incidents in which they created intentional spills. Smith, as though he was telling a story about a fraternity prank, told a story about how he and Carbeck had taken a cargo van out at night with fifty-five-gallon drums of diesel fuel. Then Smith dumped the drums through a hole in the floor of the van. Smith and Carbeck laughed when they related how the empty drums and Smith were rolling around in the back of the van as Carbeck drove away from one of the dumping sites. (Later, they would anonymously report the spills to their clients, and Hi-Po would clean them up.)

Ironically, I suspect, in this conversation, Smith and Carbeck were trying to recruit Cainstraight to be a full-fledged member of their criminal conspiracy, and Cainstraight was recording their recruitment pitch. In my experience, I had never heard—nor heard of—a recorded statement that was so incriminating regarding so many criminal acts. It was as though it had been scripted. One statement by Smith became notorious, "My scams are 90 percent foolproof."

In October 1998, the Assistant U.S. Attorney (AUSA) Kris Dighe decided to get a search warrant for the Hi-Po facility. The search warrant was executed by the task force and officers from the UM Department of Public Safety. A huge amount of records were seized, and the UM Department of Public

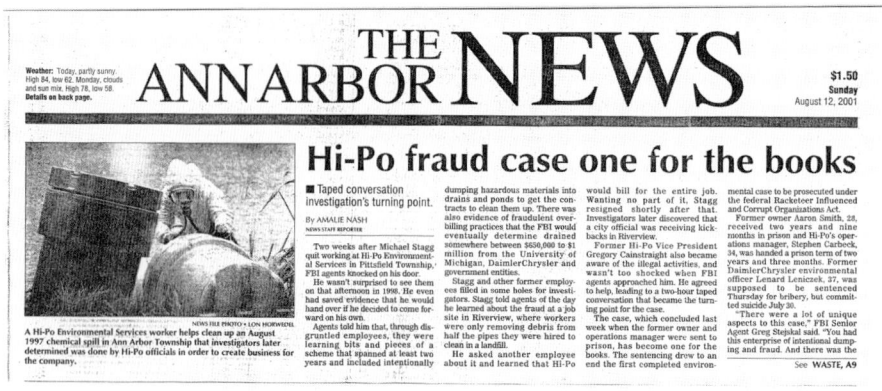

Frontpage coverage of the Hi-Po environmental fraud case (2001). *Courtesy of the* Ann Arbor *(MI)* News.

Safety arranged for space where the records could be stored and analyzed. The records would corroborate what many witnesses would tell us, and they also substantiated much of Smith and Carbeck's recorded admissions.

AUSA Dighe obtained an indictment charging Smith and Carbeck with numerous violations, including those of RICO (racketeer influenced corrupt organization, 18 USC § 1961 et seq.), a statute designed to prosecute organized crime, which, in effect, Hi-Po had become. They were also charged with the predicate acts underlying a RICO charge: mail fraud, conspiracy, bribery, money laundering and intentional dumping of hazardous waste (violations of the Clean Water Act).

So, that is what brought me to that field in Southern Michigan to see a forlorn van with a hole in the floor. The van wasn't a critical piece of evidence, but it was a symbol of the "foolproof" nature of Smith's scams.

Epilogue

Smith and Carbeck pleaded guilty to one count each of violating the RICO Act. (I'm sure they were not enthusiastic about the prospect of hearing the recorded admissions played for a trial jury.) They were the first people in the United States to ever be convicted of racketeering in an environmental case. Smith was sentenced to thirty-three months in prison, and Carbeck was given twenty-seven months. (They had both previously agreed to testify, if necessary, against other defendants.) Smith, Carbeck and Hi-Po were ordered jointly to pay a total of $504,000 restitution to UM, Chrysler, the City of Riverview, the Budd Co. and the Michigan Department of Environmental Quality. Smith was also ordered to forfeit $500,000. Both Smith and Carbeck were also ordered to publish apologies in local newspapers. They at least indicated that they were 100 percent sorry.

21
A HAPPY ENDING FOR LAW ENFORCEMENT IN A SPA CRACKDOWN

In 1999, the Ann Arbor Police Department (AAPD) Deputy Chief Craig Roderick came to me with a proposal. AAPD wanted to know if the FBI would be willing to help investigate Asian spas in Ann Arbor and prosecute them federally. At the time, I was the senior agent in the Ann Arbor FBI office and knew next to nothing about Asian spas. I was not even aware there were five such spas operating in the city and that they were actually fronts for brothels.

I consulted with the local U.S. attorney's office (USAO) and FBIHQ. I got the go-ahead and learned there were other similar cases being pursued elsewhere in the country. Further, there were national implications involved, for example, organized crime, indentured servitude, immigrant smuggling and sexual exploitation, which the then–U.S. Attorney General Janet Reno made a priority. I went back to AAPD and told them we could pursue the spas federally but only if AAPD was willing to commit to a long-term investigation. To AAPD's credit, it made that commitment. (We code named the case Seoul Provider, as most of the spas were owned and operated by South Koreans.)

These types of spas still operate around the country and exploit vulnerable women and degrade communities. We cannot ignore them. But what is particularly nice about this story is how the FBI and the local police worked so well together, and in the end, the police department reaped the financial rewards from forfeitures.

From the onset of the case, the AAPD understood that the spas/brothels could be shut down easily, like the speakeasies of the Prohibition era, but to have any lasting impact, the owners had to be identified and prosecuted. It was relatively easy to show that there was prostitution occurring in these in these spas, but the trick (no pun intended) was to prove the owners had knowledge of the prostitution and were profiting from it.

All the spas in Ann Arbor were run by Korean Americans, and surveillance and telephone pen registers indicated some interaction between spas in Ann Arbor and all over the country. All of the spas that we became aware of in Michigan and Ohio were run by Korean Americans. All of these spas had a similar operating procedures. The working girls were almost exclusively Asian, lived on the premises and seldom left. They moved from one spa to another after six weeks to two months. The spas were usually managed by older Asian women who were, in effect, madams. Often, the spas would have the "working girls" sign agreements as independent contractors, thus helping give the owners plausible deniability of knowledge of sexual activity. The working girls were, in almost all cases, uncooperative with law enforcement and could not be relied on as potential witnesses. Despite them being exploited, most had limited skills or English language abilities and were in indentured servitude status. Life was not good by American standards, but it was pretty good compared to what they had come from.

The AAPD did most of the surveillance work and the "trash pulls" that were integral to the investigation. Detective Sergeant Tom Seyfried was in charge of the AAPD Special Investigations Unit (SIU) and did a great job in coordinating the surveillances, trash pulls, et cetera. We learned that there were connections between the Ann Arbor spas and spas in Toledo, Ohio; some of the working girls were transported between them. Consequently, the SIU officers who were conducting surveillance sometimes had to cross state lines. To alleviate any jurisdictional issues, we had the SIU officers deputized as U.S. Marshals.

We did not target the working girls, nor were any them arrested or prosecuted. We also never used the technique of having an undercover officer solicit sex acts from the working girls. We were able to establish that prostitution was occurring from the trash pulls and by interviewing some of the customers who we identified from our surveillances of the spas. We did send an undercover female officer into one of the spas, but she was turned away. They were apparently not interested in female patrons who were just there for a massage.

The spas operated seven days a week with unusually long hours; for example, most were open from 10:00 a.m. to 2:00 a.m., not the kind of hours observed in legitimate massage parlors. The spas would set fees such as forty-five dollars for a half hour and sixty dollars for an hour. Generally, these initial fees went to the house. The money for sex was added to the initial fee and was negotiated based on the sexual activity. The money for sex was split between the house and the girls. All of the spas we investigated accepted credit cards. This turned out to be a key element in proving the owners had knowledge of the prostitution, as the owners had to establish the merchant account in order to accept credit cards. Thus, all proceeds from the credit cards went directly to the owner. So, if a customer were to pay his initial fee with a credit card and then, within ten or fifteen minutes, have a second charge in excess of one hundred dollars made on the card, it was obvious what was occurring and difficult for the owner to argue that they had no knowledge of the sexual activity. (All of the credit transaction information was obtained via subpoena.) What we learned was that these spas/brothels were extremely profitable, with very few legitimate massages being given.

This, coupled with physical surveillance, which included "trash pulls" (the trash pulls revealed, among other things, used condoms and daily business records) and evidence obtained when we ultimately executed search warrants, resulted in all of the spa owners being convicted of federal felony

Courtesy of the Ann Arbor *(MI)* News, *September 2, 2006.*

Courtesy of the Ann Arbor *(MI)* News, *2006.*

charges. Most of these charges were based on interstate transportation in aid of racketeering (ITAR), a prostitution statute (18USC §1952), but there were also immigration statute violations that were applicable. Also, if the owners were not U.S. citizens, they were subject to deportation on conviction.

To the best of my knowledge, there are no Asian spas/massage parlors currently operating in Ann Arbor, nor have there been any since our investigation concluded. The reward for AAPD's commitment to the long-term investigation was about $1 million in criminal forfeiture of the proceeds seized from the convicted owners.

Yes, for law enforcement, it was a happy ending.

22

ROBIN HOOD IN REVERSE

A $1.1 Million Scam

In 2005, Female Jones (not her real name), an indigent woman living in public housing in Ann Arbor, Michigan, discovered she was not eligible for federal housing assistance. The reason she was not eligible was because it appeared she was already receiving "Section 8" voucher payments. Jones wasn't aware of receiving any assistance, so it was assumed that there was a bureaucratic snafu. But an investigation revealed something far more nefarious.

Section 8 vouchers are so called because they are authorized under Section 8 of the Federal Housing Act of 1937, part of the New Deal legislation that was designed to help people who were suffering the effects of the Great Depression. In 1974, the Housing Act was amended to create the Section 8 voucher program. Low-income people were eligible for vouchers that would pay a percentage of their rent in approved housing facilities. The money for the program was to be provided by U.S. Department of Housing and Urban Development (HUD), but the program was to be administered by the state and local public housing agencies. There was only a limited amount of funding available, so not all eligible people would receive vouchers. In Michigan, a waiting list existed, and waits of three to six years were not uncommon.

The voucher payments were made directly to the indigent tenants' landlords to minimize the opportunity for fraud. Housing voucher agents working for the state prepared the application forms for the indigent applicants. These agents obtained background information and determined whether the applicants met the eligibility requirements.

Female Jones's caseworker determined that she was enrolled in the Section 8 program and that voucher payments were being sent to Washtenaw Payee Services, a company that appeared to receive Section 8 payments on behalf of several landlords in Washtenaw County. Because the woman was unaware of the payments and they were not being received by her landlord, the caseworker reported the problem to the Michigan State Housing Development Authority (MSHDA).

MSHDA's initial investigation indicated that there might be some fraudulent activity involved. As the Section 8 program is federally funded, they reported their concerns to the FBI, and a joint FBI-MSHDA investigation was opened.

Although Washtenaw Payment Services (WPS) appeared to have an office with a street address, it turned out to be a private mailbox service, which is often a red flag in a fraud investigation. The bank records for WPS were obtained via subpoena. Those records showed that WPS was formed in 1990, when LaToya Cotton filed business papers with Washtenaw County and opened a bank account. Since 1994, about eleven years, WPS had been receiving Section 8 voucher payments that were ostensibly for landlords of low-income tenants enrolled in the program. The striking thing in the filing was that the founder of WPS, LaToya Cotton, was a Michigan housing agent responsible for enrolling prospective low-income applicants for Section 8 vouchers. But even more troubling, it did not appear that any money had been paid from the WPS account to any landlords on behalf of the Section 8 enrollees.

LaToya Cotton became a Michigan housing agent for MSHDA in 1994. Very soon thereafter, she concocted her scheme. Prior to becoming a housing agent, Cotton had set up the WPS account for a legitimate purpose. But after becoming an agent and enrolling applicants for the Section 8 program, she designated WPS as the recipient for some of the applicants' landlord payments. When the WPS applicants were approved for Section 8 payments, Cotton did not tell them they had been approved. Rather, she told them they were not approved or that they were on the waitlist. None of those enrollees were ever aware that they had been approved for Section 8 payments.

In September 2005, the FBI obtained a search warrant for Cotton's office. The records seized revealed that, during the eleven years Cotton had been a housing agent, she had enrolled hundred of Section 8 applicants. Of those applicants, she designated WPS as the recipient of landlord payments for about forty of them. Cotton would periodically change the WPS enrollees,

Housing agent accused of embezzling

Officials say woman defrauded state of more than $1 million

BY AMALIE NASH
News Staff Reporter

Federal authorities have accused a Washtenaw County registered housing agent with defrauding the state of more than $1 million in funds designed to assist low-income residents with housing.

Documents recently unsealed, by federal agents charge that LaToya Cotton falsely created eligible clients to receive the state funding, which was instead paid to a company Cotton founded herself. As a housing choice voucher agent for the Michigan State Housing Development Authority in Washtenaw County, Cotton was responsible for signing up and administering candidates for programs like Section 8 housing.

Cotton's downtown Ypsilanti office was raided by federal agents Sept. 13, and MSHDA officials said her ties to the agency were severed that day. She had been a housing agent for at least 11 years.

Cotton's attorney, Timothy McDaniel of Ann Arbor, said he had seen a copy of the search warrant affidavit but was still gathering information about the investigation.

"We're moving as quickly as we can to review everything carefully," McDaniel said Tuesday. "These are all allegations, and nothing has been proven."

Cotton has not been charged with a crime and couldn't be reached for comment.

According to federal documents, a probe into Cotton's work with the agency was

SEE COTTON, BACK PAGE

Courtesy of the Ann Arbor *(MI)* News, *October 12, 2005.*

removing some and adding others. At the time her office was searched, she had eight enrollees whose voucher payments were going to WPS.

All of the money that had been paid into the WPS account was used by Cotton for personal expenses. Over Cotton's eleven-year period of fraud, the total amount paid into the account was $1,051,701. With that money, she purchased cars and went on vacations. In April 2004, Cotton purchased a 5,237-square-foot home for $830,000. MSHDA figured that the amount embezzled by Cotton could have subsidized housing for fifty families for more than four years.

In January 2006, in front of U.S. District Court Judge Patrick Duggan (the father of current Detroit mayor Mike Duggan, who, ironically, has been trying to turn Detroit around after it has been racked by years of public corruption), Cotton pleaded guilty to a federal indictment charging her with theft from a federally funded program.

Judge Duggan, in May 2006, sentenced Cotton to three and a half years incarceration, three years supervised release, and ordered her to pay $1.1 million in restitution. (Cotton's house was forfeited and sold, with the proceeds used to pay a portion of the restitution.)

At the time, I was quoted as saying, "She [Cotton] was living in a mansion, and there were low-income people who should have been receiving Section 8 housing subsidies. It was Robin Hood in reverse."

23

RETIREMENT AND A COLD MURDER CASE IN DETROIT DATING BACK TO 1857

On Halloween 2006, I retired from the FBI. Federal law enforcement has a mandatory retirement age of fifty-seven, but I was given a six-month extension by Director Robert Mueller. I always wanted to be an FBI agent, and after becoming an agent, it is all I wanted to do. So, I stayed as long as I could—thirty-one years and eight months.

As I was packing up the things in my office, I reread an 1857 reward poster that my wife had found at an estate sale in Ann Arbor. My wife had the poster framed, and it had long hung next to my desk. It reminded me of a possibly apocryphal story.

Ernest Hemingway was having lunch with some writer friends when he proposed a wager. He bet ten dollars that he could write a story in six words. With, no doubt, some curiosity, everyone at the table put ten dollars in the pot. Hemingway wrote on a napkin, "For sale: baby shoes, never worn." Hemingway passed the napkin around the table and collected his winnings. Hemingway's six-word story is an extreme example of what is called "flash fiction." My experience with flash fiction was that old reward poster.

The poster had a place, Detroit, and a date of April 14, 1857, and it was offering "$1,500 Reward!" for information regarding a missing man, "John Rodgers, a resident of the town of Farmington, age 27." The poster provides a physical description of John Rodgers and the clothing he was wearing when he was last seen leaving "Finney's Hotel stable at dusk Tuesday evening, April 7th [1857]," where he left a span, or pair, of horses. The poster also indicates a suspicion of "foul play" and offers $1,000 "for the detection

$1,500 REWARD!

MISSING!

JOHN RODGERS, a resident of the town of Farmington, 27 years old, six feet high, weighs about 160 pounds, heavy head of dark hair, heavy dark sandy whiskers, heavy eyebrows, dark blue eyes. Left Finney's Hotel stable at dusk Tuesday evening, April 7th, and has not been seen or heard of since. He was a farmer, retiring in his habits, and a man of few words. Had on a gray colored coat with black velvet collar, (no overcoat,) dark blue pants, kip skin boots and a black Kossuth hat. Left a span of horses in said stable, and has probably met with foul play. I will pay

ONE THOUSAND DOLLARS

for the detection of any person or persons who may have been guilty of the murder of said John Rodgers, and

FIVE HUNDRED DOLLARS

for the finding or recovery of the body, or ONE THOUSAND DOLLARS for the finding and recovery of said John Rodgers, if alive.

Detroit, April 14, 1857.   **STEPHEN RODGERS.**

An 1857 reward poster. *Author's collection.*

of any person or persons who may have been guilty of the murder of John Rodgers." The reward is offered by Stephen Rodgers.

Like Hemingway's baby shoes, the poster doesn't so much tell a story as it suggests one. I have often wondered about the fate of John Rodgers and what clues were contained on the poster. The thing that stands out is the reward amount, "$1,500." In 1857, $1,500 was an exceptionally large amount of money, worth about $42,000 today. It isn't clear who Stephen Rodgers was from the poster, but he must have been a man of some means.

Since receiving the poster, I have made sporadic inquiries of local historians and checked records, trying to find the rest of the story behind the poster. Lee Peel, a historian of Farmington, Michigan, was able to determine that Stephen and John Rodgers were prosperous farmers with land in Farmington, but he wasn't able to find any information regarding the incident described in the poster.

Later, I happened on an article in the *Detroit Free Press* about the abolitionist movement and the rise of the Republican Party in Michigan. In the article, Seymour Finney was mentioned. In the 1850s, Finney was an abolitionist who ran a hotel in Detroit. Behind the hotel, he had a large barn on the northeast corner of State and Griswold Streets. (Today, there is a historical marker there.) Finney used the barn to hide runaway enslaved people until they could cross the Detroit River into Canada. The barn was located just blocks from the river. Canada was a haven for the erstwhile enslaved people because, in 1837, England had abolished slavery throughout its empire. So, any enslaved person who made it to Canada was free.

In the 1840s and 1850s, an Underground Railroad developed in the United States. Enslaved people followed established routes to northern states, where they were relatively safe. Some of those routes led from the South to Michigan, where there were many sympathetic people willing to hide escapees and aid their passage to Canada. In fact, the Republican Party, which was established by people who were opposed to the expansion of slavery beyond the states where it existed, began to flourish in Michigan. The party's first statewide convention was held in Jackson, Michigan, in 1854. One of the party's founders was Dr. Nathan Thomas, who had a medical practice in Kalamazoo and maintained a "station" on the Underground Railroad in Kalamazoo.

There were also free Black people in Michigan who were active in the Underground Railroad. George de Baptiste, a freedman, owned a barbershop and a bakery in Detroit. He also owned a steamship named *T. Whitney*, which transported freight and passengers from Detroit to Windsor, Canada. The *T. Whitney* also surreptitiously smuggled escaped enslaved people to Canada at de Baptiste's direction. De Baptiste had formed a secret organization, African American Mysteries, or Order of the Men of Oppression, which worked with the Underground Railroad. Seymour Finney, as a "conductor" on the Underground Railroad, would have been a member or an affiliate member of the secret organization.

Secrecy was necessary because in 1850, the Fugitive Slave Act was enacted by Congress. The act required that escaped enslaved people be apprehended anywhere in the United States, including "free" states, and returned to their masters. Rewards were offered for enslaved people, and despite there being many people in Michigan who were opposed to slavery, there were many who were not or who were out to collect a reward. On occasion, slavecatchers stayed in Finney's Hotel, while enslaved people were hidden in the barn.

So, John Rodgers was last seen leaving "Finney's Hotel stable at dusk." Had he stumbled across some fugitive enslaved people? Did he attempt to obstruct their escape, or did he try to resist the efforts of bounty hunters to apprehend them?

Recently, I talked to a Detroit historian named Bill Loomis about the poster. Loomis has access to Detroit newspaper archives. (I had previously had other people with access to newspaper archives search for anything relating to John Rodgers's disappearance with no success.) Loomis was able to find one article in the *Detroit Free Press*, dated May 21, 1857, titled "Verdict in Rodgers Case." The article is not about a trial but an inquest held in the office of Justice Ensworth, presumably acting as coroner. John Rodgers's body had been recovered from the Detroit River, but it is not clear from the article when it was recovered. The reward poster was dated April 14, seven days after he went missing, and the inquest occurred on May 20.

One witness at the inquest was the father of the deceased, Stephen Rodgers, who offered the reward. Mr. Rodgers testified that he and John had come to the city with a load of pork, which was sold. The father kept the proceeds from the sale, except for six dollars, which he gave to his son John between 1:00 p.m. and 2:00 p.m. Rodgers said that he thought his son had between twenty-five and one hundred dollars in his possession and that he had two "porte-monnaies," or wallets, with him—a new one and an old one. No money was found with the body.

When Rodgers gave his son the money, he noticed some men standing on the corner nearby. "There were from four to six men and they were talking with one another. I noticed particularly one of them looking at us. They had the appearance of rather hard cases. I never saw them before neither have I seen them since." Also testifying at the inquest was a Dr. Terry, who was apparently the medical examiner. He had done an analysis of the deceased's stomach, which had been delivered to him the day before in a jar. (In a time before refrigeration, this evokes some unsavory images.) Dr. Terry determined that John Rodgers's last meal consisted of corned beef and potatoes. Due to the state of digestion, Dr. Terry believed Rodgers died around two to three hours after his last meal.

Dr. Terry testified that he had conducted "chemical tests to the contents of the stomach to ascertain whether opium or any of its preparations were present, including morphine or its salts, but nothing of the kind was detected. [This seems to infer that, at that time, if poisoning was suspected, the drug of choice was an opiate.] The time that has elapsed since the death of Mr. Rodgers would render the detection of a vegetable poison difficult if not impossible."

Dr. Terry concluded: "I would say, that in regard to Mr. Rodgers' death, it strikes me that the theory assumed by the physicians on the post mortem examination, that is, that the deceased was drugged is the most probable one. The absence of opium or morphine in the contents of the stomach at such a length of time after his death is no disproof of this supposition."

The verdict of the jury was:

> *The jury upon their oaths present that from the appearance of the body and from all the facts and circumstances disclosed by the testimony, they are of the opinion that said Rodgers came to death in the city of Detroit by unlawful means, used by persons or persons unknown to the jurors who are unable definitely to determine from the testimony before them what means in fact were used by the murderers to effect their diabolical purpose.*

So, the jury concluded that Rodgers was murdered, but they didn't know how, why or by whom. Like the unused baby shoes, several possibilities are suggested. I will continue to search for the rest of the story, but for now, at least I know John Rodgers's fate.

BIBLIOGRAPHY

Burnstein, Scott M. *Motor City Mafia*. Charleston, SC: Arcadia Publishing, 2006.
Burrough, Bryan. *Public Enemies: America's Greatest Crime Wave and the Birth of the FBI, 1933–34*. London: Penguin Books, 2009.
Goldsmith, Jack. *In Hoffa's Shadow*. New York: Farrar, Straus and Giroux, 2019.
Hunt, Don. "The Controversial Verdicts." *Ann Arbor Observer* 2, no. 5 (September 1977): 1.
Reynolds, Quentin. *The F.B.I.* Landmark Books. London: Random House, 1954.

INDEX

A

Akfirat, John 53, 54
Alcohol, Tobacco and Firearms, Bureau of (ATF) 62, 119
Alkhabaz, Jacob 113
American Revolution 119
Ann Arbor, Michigan 15, 22, 23, 27, 46, 47, 50, 53, 55, 59, 63, 67, 78, 79, 84, 88, 114, 126, 128, 131, 132, 136, 137, 139, 140, 143
Ann Arbor Police Department (AAPD) 68
Atkinson, Rick (author, *The Long Gray Line*) 132
Atlanta Federal Penitentiary 82, 83

B

Baker, Jake 113, 114, 115
Barringer, Daniel (Barringer Crater) 128
Biden, Joseph 111
Bisceglie, Anthony 61, 62, 63
Bivens, Webster 65, 66, 71
Bloom, Lloyd 57
Bonds, Barry 112
Brennan, Jim 56
bribery 19, 134
Burnstein, Scott 38, 149

C

Cainstraight, Greg 132, 133
Canseco, Jose 107, 110, 111
Carbeck, Stephen 131, 132, 133, 134, 135
Carr, Lloyd 58
Clingingsmith, Jack 72, 73, 74, 75
Cohn, Avern 115, 117
Collins, Steven 128, 129, 130

INDEX

Combined DNA Index System (CODIS) 30
conspiracy 27, 28, 29, 38, 40, 68, 69, 70, 73, 74, 75, 94, 98, 102, 121, 123, 133, 134
Convertino, Rick 40
Cordes, Keith 38
Corrado, Anthony "the Bull" 38, 40
Cotton, LaToya 141, 142
Craig, Jerry 90
Criminal Justice Information Services (CJIS) 31

D

Davidson, William "Bill" 52, 53, 54
Debs, Richard 99, 102
Decker, Michigan 122, 123
Degan, Dennis 106
Delonis, Richard "Dick" 23, 26
Detroit, Michigan 15, 16, 18, 19, 20, 21, 32, 36, 37, 38, 40, 41, 43, 44, 45, 46, 48, 52, 79, 82, 88, 91, 106, 115, 123, 132, 142, 143, 144, 145, 146, 147
Diablo, Canyon Meteor Crater 126, 127, 128, 129
Dighe, Kris 133, 134
DNA 30
Drug Enforcement Administration (DEA) 66, 74
drug trafficking 66, 69, 70, 79, 110
Duggan, Patrick 142

E

Environmental Protection Agency (EPA) 131
Equine 57, 106, 107, 110, 111
Escanaba, Michigan 86, 87, 88, 89, 90, 91, 92, 93
Esposito, James "Jim" 18

F

fingerprints 30, 31, 32, 33, 96, 102
Fischetti, Lou 56
Flattery, Steve 132
Flynn, Molly 61, 62
Foldes, Francis 24
Food and Drug Administration (FDA) 106, 110
Ford, John (director, *The Man Who Shot Liberty Valance* and *The Long Gray Line*) 59, 132
Ford Motor Company 52
fraud 19, 53, 54, 106, 134, 140, 141, 142
Freeh, Louis "Louie" 60
free speech 113

G

Garrity, Robert "Bob" 18
General Motors 45, 72, 99
Giacalone, Tony 17, 20, 21
Giacalone, Vito 21, 38
Gittleson, Mike 104, 105, 106, 107, 110, 112
Grand Rapids, Michigan 15
Grassley, Charles "Chuck" 111

INDEX

Gray, Jesse 100, 101, 102, 103
Guttler, Richard "Dick" 26

H

Hallinan, Kevin 110, 111
Hancock, Steve 90
Harlow, Bob 100, 101, 102
Harrison, Mike 61
Heilbrunn, Paul 76, 77, 78
Heilbrunn, Richard 76
Hill, Anne 23
Hill, James Frederick 79, 81
Hi-Po 132, 133, 134
Hoffa, Jimmy 15, 16, 18, 20, 44
Holloway, Donald 73, 74, 75
Hoover, J. Edgar 31, 36
Horvath, Greg 132
Howard, Juwan 56

K

Kaczynski, David 60, 61
Kaczynski, Linda 60, 61
Kaczynski, Ted 60, 61, 63, 64, 114
Kalamazoo, Michigan 145
Kaszubski, Dave 106
Kelleher, Tom 48
Koernke, Mark 94, 95, 96, 97, 98
Koresh, David 120, 121

L

Lansing, Michigan 15
Lapekas, Stan 47
Leary, Linda 76, 77, 81

Leibson, Michael "Mike" 106
Lindsay, Paul 33, 35
Loonsfoot, Vincent 86, 87, 88, 90, 91, 92, 93, 106
Love, Tom 55

M

Macomb County, Michigan 37
mafia 16, 18, 19, 20, 21, 36, 38, 66, 67, 149
Mandarich, Tony 104
Manuel, Warde 56
Marquette, Michigan 15, 86, 88, 91, 92
Martin, Eddie 56
McConnell, James 60, 62, 63
McGwire, Mark 107, 108, 111, 112
McNulty, Kevin 126, 128, 129
McVeigh, Timothy 95, 121, 122, 123, 124, 125
Menth, Thomas 30, 31, 32, 33, 34, 35
Michigan Militia 98
Michigan State Police 38, 74, 95, 100
Michigan State University 74, 95, 100, 104, 110, 132, 141
Michigan, University of 22, 52, 53, 60, 62, 67, 68, 70, 94, 113, 126, 131, 133
MLB 56, 57, 110, 111, 112
money laundering 134
Moore, Michael (director, *Roger and Me*) 74
Moss, Joel 62, 63
murder 16, 18, 20, 27, 28, 31, 32, 34, 35, 44, 92, 95, 128, 137, 144

INDEX

N

Narciso, Filipina 25, 26, 27, 28, 29
NBA 52, 56, 110
NCAA 56, 57, 77, 110
Nebraska, University of 12, 55, 157
Nemo's Bar 19
NFL 56, 110
NHL 56, 110
Nichols, James 123
Nichols, Terry 122, 123
Nicolay, Ingo 73, 74, 75

O

Oakland County, Michigan 16, 48
Oklahoma City Bombing 8, 95, 119, 121, 122
Omaha (NE) Central High School 12, 157
organized crime 16, 36, 66, 67, 134, 136

P

Papson, Albert, Jr. 67, 68
Perez, Leonara 25, 26, 27, 28, 29
postal inspectors 62
Pratt, Philip 28, 29
prostitution 137, 139

Q

Quantico, Virginia 13, 14, 15, 63, 110
Quassarano, Rafaillo "Jimmy Q" 37
Quinn, T.J. 111

R

Racketeer Influenced Corrupt Organization (RICO) 134
racketeering 20, 40, 102, 134
Randall, William "Bill" 90, 91, 106, 107
Redd, Christian 111
Reno, Janet 60, 121, 136
robbery 45, 96, 98
Roderick, Craig 136
Rodriguez, Alex 112
Rotary Club of Ann Arbor 158
Ruggirello, Antonio "T.R." 37
Ruggirello, Luigi "Louie the Bulldog" 37
Russo, Dan 26

S

Salvation Army 82, 83, 84, 85
Schembechler, Bo 55, 56, 68, 104, 111, 112
Schrope, Rick 69
Sczesny, Ed 52, 53, 54
Seyfried, Tom 137
Shanahan, Hugh 56
Shedd, James 78
Shure, Fred 67
Shure, Ned 67
Sidetrack Bar & Grill 78
Smiley, Jim 63
Smith, Aaron 131
Smith, Chuck 90
Smith, Roger 74
Sosa, Sammy 112
Sprague, Michael Lee 30, 31, 32, 33, 34, 35

INDEX

Stagg, Michael 132
Stempel, Robert 45, 46
steroids 57, 58, 104, 105, 106, 107, 108, 110, 111, 112
Stewart, Jimmy 12, 59
surveillance 16, 36, 37, 40, 42, 43, 47, 63, 66, 67, 68, 107, 120, 128, 137, 138
Swanson, Susan 61
SWAT 82, 83, 88, 89, 90, 92, 93, 106, 123

T

Tanceusz, James Gregory 67, 68, 70
Teamsters 16, 18, 19, 20, 21
theft 50, 54, 75, 128, 129, 142
Timberland Game Ranch 37, 38, 40
Tocco, Giacomo "Jack" 37, 38, 40, 41
Torgler, Marty 56
Turner Diaries, The 121

U

Unabomber 59, 60, 61, 63, 64, 114
Upper Peninsula 86

W

Waco, Texas 119, 122
Wallace, Mike 111
Walters, Norby 57
Ward, Gene 23, 94
Washtenaw County, Michigan 37, 114, 132, 141
Wayne County, Michigan 33
Welch, Neil 16, 36
Wenzlaff, Curtis 107, 108, 111
Williams, Clinton 48
Williams, Thurman 32, 45, 46
Willow Run 99, 100
Wilson, Darryl 45, 46, 47, 48
World War II 11, 99

Y

Yanko, Richard 26
Ypsilanti, Michigan 78, 99, 100

ABOUT THE AUTHOR

Greg Stejskal was born and raised in Omaha, Nebraska. He graduated from Omaha Central High School (the oldest high school in Nebraska and still going strong) and attended the University of Nebraska in Lincoln (UNL) on a football scholarship. After obtaining his bachelor's degree, he attended the UNL College of Law. He received his Juris Doctorate in 1974.

Greg entered on duty as an FBI special agent in March 1975. After completing new agent training at the FBI Academy, Quantico, Virginia, Greg was assigned to the Detroit Division (Michigan). Except for in-service training and temporary duty (TDY) assignments, his entire career with the FBI was in Michigan. He initially worked in Detroit on several different squads. In 1981, he was assigned to the Ann Arbor Resident Agency, a satellite office of Detroit. In 1995, he was designated the senior resident agent (SRA) of the Ann Arbor RA, a position he held until his retirement in 2006.

During his career, Greg worked numerous violations of federal law within the FBI's jurisdiction and participated in many high-profile investigations. Greg was also a member of the FBI Detroit Special Weapons and Tactics (SWAT) team from 1977 to 1998.

About the Author

After retirement, Greg began writing columns and stories for *Tickle-the-Wire*, a federal law enforcement blog. Several other publications have run his stories. He has also been interviewed by documentarians, podcasters and the University of Michigan NPR affiliate about FBI investigations.

Greg continues to live in Ann Arbor, Michigan, with his wife, Pat, a retired kindergarten teacher. They have two adult children, Taryn and Andrew "Andy"—both graduates of the University of Michigan.

Greg and Pat are both actively involved in community service. Greg was the president of the Rotary Club of Ann Arbor (RCAA) from 2018 to 2019 (RCAA is the largest Rotary Club in Michigan).

Visit us at
www.historypress.com